the
RelationOGRAPHER™

*bruce*hudson

The art of relationship marketing

Powerful strategies for transforming lifelong
customers into *generational clients.*

*bruce*hudson

Published by **the RelationOGRAPHER**
*bruce*hudson

Manufactured in the United States of America

Forward

The first time I met Bruce, he looked like a school boy in a grown-up man's shirt and slacks, his face was literally glowing with excitement as he and his late wife Sue shot dozens of photos of me and my young son Isaiah. He had the apple cheeks of youth and enough energy for three people. I knew when we left the photo studio that I had not only met some wonderful photographers, but wonderful people that I wanted to remain friends with.

Bruce and I are both natural "extroverts"....we get our emotional batteries charged by being connected to others. We never tire of meeting new people or forming new friendships. But whether you are a "people person" like Bruce and I are, or more withdrawn and need alone time to recharge, the principals in this book will help you to grow your business and focus on your clients, no matter what your natural bent is, or even what your chosen profession is.

Bruce has learned how to market, without manipulating, how to form and keep relationships with his customer base, not to exploit but to better meet their needs. He not only communicates effectively, he does it honestly and thoughtfully.

Bruce Hudson is a creative ball of energy. The thing that impresses me most about him is that when he figures out a new or better way to approach something, whether it is a better way to shoot a photo of a blushing bride, or a better way to display the photos in a session with wine and soft music, he doesn't keep his discoveries under lock and key! He is not only willing, but eager to teach the methods and techniques he has found successful to any who want to gain the knowledge! Like an apple tree laden with crisp, red apples in the fall, Bruce shares the fruits of his discoveries with anyone who happens by and is eager to learn and grow.

It's been almost 20 years since I first met Bruce, and despite the salt and pepper hair, he still appears to me as a school boy in an adult world, his energy and passion is contagious!

May this book help you to understand the value of staying connected and serving those who might turn to you for a product or service. My staff at the Delilah show always tries to remember that our audience listens because they know we care about them. Bruce Hudson has the same attitude about his clients that we do in our radio studio, he believes in staying connected.

Delilah

Meet Bruce Hudson
The Relationographer

Seattle area native Bruce Hudson has led a colorful and diverse life. His photographic career started like many professionals, as a hobby in high school. Bruce's major interests back in the early 70's were playing trumpet in the nationally award-winning Kent Meridian high school jazz band, and his first love, Sue Crum, who inspired his artistic direction in photography, both in front of the camera and in the darkroom!

This changed when Bruce and Sue married in 1975 and Bruce began his junior year at Western Washington University. Music and music education was still the focus by day, but the love for photography and photographing people took up the evenings and weekends with weddings of fellow college students and friends. After graduating from college in 1978, Bruce started a career as a high school band director, not far from his childhood home in Maple Valley, Washington. During those musical years he had the opportunity to play with such greats as Bob Hope, Oscar Peterson, and Kenny G.

Even though teaching music was a full-time job, Bruce and Sue still embraced photography as a major part of their lives. They continued to photograph weddings and portraits on weekends for fun and to help supplement their income.

After working part-time out of their home for four years, Bruce decided to leave teaching, and they opened their first store-front studio in 1982. The early studio years were challenging due to the recession in '82 and ultra-high interest rates. Bruce and Sue pretty much photographed everything: pets, passports, dances, sports leagues, seniors, weddings, families, and children. During this time they also started a family with Josh being born in '82 and McKenna in '84. The Hudson's also became serious students of marketing, reading every book on the subject and then utilizing the concepts in their growing business. All that study and hard work paid off big-time!

As the business, clientele, and income grew, so did the number of photographic awards locally, nationally, and internationally. In 1993, Bruce and Sue won the first wedding album competition and the grand award print with the first perfect "100" score at the national meeting of Wedding and Portrait Photographers International.

The next 10 years took Bruce and Sue all over the country sharing their successful photographic and business strategies to thousands of studio owners at conventions, seminars, and workshops.

In 1994, during a routine exam, a cancerous mole was found under Sue's left arm. It was removed, but 22 months later, on February 17, 1996, Sue Hudson passed away at the age of 41. Bruce and the kids established a memorial scholarship fund in Sue's name, and each year give a number of scholarships to professional photography schools throughout the country.

Today, despite the loss of Sue, Bruce still holds a passion for business, marketing and the photographic profession. In many ways, he's written this book as a part of Sue's legacy, sharing their journey in growing a business.

Bruce holds a Master Craftsman degree from the Professional Photographers of America and is one of only 40 active members in the prestigious organization Cameracraftsmen of America. A much sought-after speaker to professional photography organizations, Bruce has lectured on behalf of Fuji Film USA, H&H Color Lab, Mamiya Cameras, Capri Albums, Marathon Press, and Excel Frames throughout the United States, New Zealand, Canada, and Puerto Rico. Over the years he has produced and authored over 25 instructional video/DVD programs dealing with portrait and wedding photography and marketing, photographed more than a thousand weddings, and made tens of thousands of family, children, and high school senior portraits since 1982. He's also had in front of his lens, President Bush (41), future Hall of Fame pitching great Randy Johnson, and night time radio celebrity Delilah and her family.

Bruce has not only been named a Master Photographer, but also referred to as a Master Marketer that specializes in Relationship Marketing and thus the Relationographer!

Acknowledgements

I've had the opportunity to teach and lecture in all fifty states except Alaska. Since my wife and soul mate Sue passed away from melanoma cancer at the age of 41 in 1996, I've started every program with a dedication to her. It's going to be the same with this book. Having the ultimate pleasure of knowing and being with her since we were high school sweethearts in the early 70's, Sue has always been and continues to be an inspiration in my life. An incredible wife and mother, and partner in business and life, she was always positive, up-beat and never gave up at anything until her final breath. She consistently strived for perfection in everything she did. In many ways this book is part of the Sue Hudson legacy.

To my amazing children, Josh and McKenna, you've been through a lot in your young lives. It's been fun watching your mother's drive and determination along with her humor and wit come through in your personalities. Your daily accomplishments and success inspire me and everyone!"

To Debbie, not only a fantastic employee but also my "day wife." Thank you for being able to assume Sue's business responsibilities and putting up with me for the last 18 years. To Kelly, thank you for having the patience and understanding during life's transitions. This book and the mechanics would not have happened without Holly, Lauren and my son Josh (The Closer). Josh has the ability to help me focus and finish all my various projects. They did everything from transcribing my thoughts to pre-editing for my editor. Thank you! And to McKenna, it was you that said, "Dad you're really good at the marketing stuff...you should write a book!" I didn't want to disappoint you daughter, so here it is!

To my long time friend and client Delilah, thank you for the inspirational forward to the book and your heart and soul on the radio nightly!

To my sister, Patty, yes we are orphans now, but I feel we get closer with each passing day. I love ya.

To all my studio team members over the years, thank you for sharing my passion of my profession and always making the client first. To my editor Kevin Conners, the confidence and patience you've given me though this educational process of writing this book has been tremendous. I knew the first day in class in San Diego we would become lifelong friends. Thank you for all your hard work!

I'm a product of many mentors throughout my 51 years that have enriched my life. Thank you to Hal Sherman, Ken Whitmire, Charles Lewis, Jim Niswonger, Paul and Joyce Highsmith, and from H & H Color Lab; Ron Fleckal, and Wayne and Shirley Haub.

To Steve Sheanin, who still to this day is a cross between a brother, father, uncle, friend and Yoda!

To Terri, you fell in love with a crazy man with a crazy life. I look forward to our life together and what the future holds. Love you, babe!

Now that the hardest part of the book is complete, let's get started!

CHAPTERS

Introduction

PHOTOGRAPHER OR MARKETING EXPERT?

"What do *you* know about marketing…you're just a photographer!"

It's true. I admit it: I'm a photographer and not a marketing expert. I love what I do; in fact, I do believe I have the best job in the world. I have the opportunity every day to capture a little slice of time—or even better yet, history—for my clients. As I begin writing this book, it's the morning after I just finished an assignment in beautiful Sun Valley, Idaho. I was asked to document a family coming together to celebrate their mother and grandmother Blanche for her 90th birthday. Wow… What an honor! Last night, as I sat at the end of the table in the formal dining room at the famous Sun Valley Lodge, I thought of all the history and famous people that dined and danced in this room through the decades. I also thought of all the history and life experiences that this extremely sharp and gracious 90-year-old woman had experienced in her lifetime. I was inspired, to say the least!

I wasn't there to just document this for the family that hired me, but also for generations of family that haven't even been born yet! What an awesome opportunity, responsibility, and yes, an honor to be a part of the celebration. Do you see why I think I have the best job in the world?

When Sue and I started Hudson's Designer Portraits in August of 1982, we had ten or so weddings on the books and a couple of leagues committed to having us photograph their teams. We had a few high school seniors check us out as well as a few families to do holiday portraits. All of this work got us through the Christmas season. It was an exciting yet scary time because our firstborn, Josh, came along in November of that year.

In January, after our first Christmas rush, it became apparent that owning a photography studio was definitely a seasonal proposition! This was our first introduction to cash flow... or lack of it. With a two-month-old now in our life, it was essential that this once-hobby-turned-profession (business) needed to begin making money, and as soon as possible.

We tried everything from phone book cover adds to coupons on the back of grocery store receipts. This was also a time in our nation's history when interest rates were a whopping 18% and the economy was in a deep recession.

With determination to succeed, Sue and I started to study businesses that seemed to survive during this economic downturn. We also started on a journey, to learn and then implement everything we could about marketing and how to create consistent cash flow.

In the next few years our studio business began to flourish and grow. We started to become well-known by other photographers in our state and later across the country for our studio marketing strategies. Prior to Sue's passing away, we had the privilege to lecture to professional photography organizations in 49 states, Canada, Puerto Rico and even New Zealand.

All of that brings us to the birth of this book. Being known for our marketing ability, my local chamber of commerce encouraged me to speak at a networking breakfast event. I tailored the talk to be more geared toward general small business instead of photographers and studio owners. The response was overwhelming and came from business owners that assumed I knew a lot more than I did about marketing. This was a true revelation. Remember, I'm just a photographer, an artist-type. What do I know about marketing a business?

PHOTOGRAPHER OR MARKETING EXPERT?

Well, over the next few pages I hope I can share what Sue and I learned in our quest to find insight into many marketing answers, especially when it comes to the relationship between you and your customer or client. I like to call it Relationship Marketing. Enjoy!

IN THE BEGINNING

As long as I can remember, I've liked to sell stuff. In cub scouts it was light bulbs. In seventh grade band it was Christmas wrapping paper for new "powder blue" band blazers for performances. I lived just up the street from my elementary school and one summer, at the age of twelve, I started a little snack bar. Almost every night that summer, there were either T-ball, baseball, or softball games played on the four fields. I'd pop popcorn, make black cherry Kool-Aid™ (my favorite), and walk to the store to purchase candy. Lots of candy. Back then "penny candy" like Smarties™ (another favorite) actually *was* a penny, so I just doubled the price to two cents. "Look" Bars were five cents, so I sold them for a dime. I found a couple of apple crates (easy, being in Washington State) and two planks for the counter, and voila! I was in business! This little venture was so successful that I sold out every night.

One of the things that I remember from this early experience was all of the repeat business. It was always the same people that would come back to buy, and even more so, visit with me. They all liked to chat and all liked to ask questions about my little business. Many also mentioned that they looked forward to the games at East Hill Field because of my snack stand!

This was my first introduction to what relationships in business are all about. It's not just the product or service you're selling; it's the experience that you deliver. In this case the *experience* was a little twelve year old entrepreneur selling stuff at little league games.

I do really feel bad for my neighbors when I was growing up. They were subjected to me coming by the house every time we had a fund raiser. Did they need all of the candy bars, candles, wrapping paper, and light bulbs? Probably not! But most looked forward to my knock on the door, perhaps because I explained in detail the reason for the fund raiser or maybe how buying my light bulbs would save them money in the long run. Maybe it was because I would ask questions about them and how their life was going. Maybe it was my customer service that sometimes included some flowers from my mother's garden.

It's amazing how many lawn mowing jobs I got out of these relationships. It's even more amazing how now some thirty-five years later, many of these same neighbors have been and continue to be photography clients! Sure, having a business for more than twenty years in an area where you grew up is likely to mean former neighbors are clients; but, I'm convinced it still comes down to the relationship that was initially formed.

So, looking back, what were some of the elements that contributed to the success of my early business encounters?

Competitive nature

Whether it was selling light bulbs, candles, Christmas wrapping paper, or whatever, there was always a prize for who sold the most. I wanted that prize! Even today, I don't know exactly what motivates me to win, but I do know that I don't like to lose.

When it comes to measuring success in selling contests, it's easy to determine a winner-- whoever sells the most stuff wins. It's like most sports—very objective. At the end of the game you have a winner--just look at the scoreboard. But when it comes to things like music or art, for instance, the measurement of success or a clear cut winner is very subjective.

IN THE BEGINNING

The competitions that have a subjective nature usually involve judges. It's always fascinated me to watch gymnastics and ice skating and how they're judged. How the judge perceived the performance is everything. I feel this is why American Idol has been so popular throughout the years. It's not just the performers and their performances but the judges' opinions – better yet, their reactions to the performance!

When Sue and I first started entering print competitions at our local Seattle area and state photography associations, we had no idea what we were doing. As the months and years went by, we observed that each of the judges on the panel saw things so differently. Some were really picky when it came to lighting, some when it came to posing or exposure or color harmony.

Judging photography, like any art form, is tough and again, very subjective. Was there anything that the judges could agree on? There was… it was creativity! Even the pickiest judge would fudge a little on the technical stuff (lighting, posing, etc.) if the print was creative and something different. Especially in that particular print competition.

A wonderful example of this was a print that I entered at state competition early on in our career. It was an image of a pregnant woman. She and her husband had been great clients, later friends. In fact, we hired her some fifteen years ago and she is currently my incredible office manager. Debbie was one of the most beautiful pregnant women I've ever had the privilege to photograph. (Of course, Sue was also in that category.) Debbie's singing background in high school and college helped her appreciate the more artsy approach to my photography. Her image had her leaning against a tall tree in a forest with the light coming through a white gauzy gown, showing off her pregnant tummy! For competition purposes, the print measured 16x20 vertical. I used lots of space, having Debbie standing full length. Her body only measured about five inches high! She was looking up at the sky in expectation of her first child.

This annual state competition had many different categories. The biggest was always "Portrait of a Woman." Family portraiture and men would have maybe eight or ten entries, but women would have over a hundred! A tough category to do well in because of the quantity of prints, or was it? One by one, each print would be judged. One beautiful close-up of a woman, after another. The judges were getting pretty tired of seeing basically the same image, just with a different face. This was demonstrated by the lackluster scores they were giving the prints. You could almost sense that the judges were just looking for something unique to reward and break the boredom. That's when my image of Debbie came up. As they read the title *("Which Will It Be...?")*, you could sense they were excited to judge something other than a close-up head shot.

The result? You probably guessed it. The print was a big hit. It took best portrait of a female, best portrait overall, and was in the running for best of show! Was it really that superior to other entries? No. It was just simply unique and different from the other prints in its category.

The lesson learned here works in *any* competitive environment. Exploit the weakness of your opponent. In football, it's the coaching staff meticulous studying the tapes of next week's team to find a lineman slow to react or a defensive back that your star receiver can easily beat.

Competitive nature: Exploiting the weakness of your opponent—
Most businesses don't maintain relationships with their existing clients!

A unique experience

Anyone can have a Kool-Aid stand. People are drawn to ideas that are unique in their own special way. Taking a little extra time to pop popcorn and go to the store to buy candy and fruit turned an ordinary Kool-Aid stand into a snack stand. This concept has echoed throughout my lifetime. In 9th grade I took first place in the science fair. It wasn't the fact that I was gifted in science, but that my project and presentation were very unique.

I've always been fascinated with space exploration. Some of my fondest memories are of waking up early to see the Mercury, Gemini, and Apollo Missions. I wanted my project to have something relating to space. But what? About this time, one of our local television stations started to have satellite weather forecasts. This was too cool. As I researched further, I was hooked.

Having a topic that I was excited about made the project fun to work on. I knew that this subject was unique enough to do well, but how could I draw the attention of the judges to win? <u>This is one of the greatest lessons I learned in business</u>: It's all in the presentation. My science fair display was awesome! I was able to draw the attention of everyone, including the judges. My graphic design teacher made some suggestions that made the signage stand out. I was also able to acquire a "reel to reel" tape of what the weather satellite sounded like when it transmitted back to earth. Once again, it wasn't just the uniqueness of the content of the project, as much as the uniqueness of the presentation! I live by this mantra every day, from projecting my images for my clients, to creating the ultimate booth for bridal shows.

After 25 years of owning a studio, not everyone in this world is excited to invest in photography. I've found, though, that the clients that are willing to invest in my work are looking for something different or unique. My first realization of this was at our first mall display in a major shopping center– I think it was a home and gardening theme. We paid $400.00 to be part of the show from Thursday to Sunday. It was a little scary, showing examples of my early portraits which we literally stolen off our studio's walls. Every sample print we owned (which wasn't many) was at the 4-day show. The studio walls were bare.

My "pride and joy" image at the time was also the biggest, a 40x60 inch print. Most people at the show had never seen a photographic portrait that large before, or experienced a photograph mounted on canvas. It was taken in the Cascade Mountains at about the five thousand foot level, with an unobstructed jaw-dropping view of Mount Rainier. The image alone without my three subjects was fantastic. When we added the mom and her two daughters, it really told a story. Imagine, mom and her two girls were dressed in white cotton gowns. The oldest girl, about seven years old, was sitting next to her mom looking at her new baby sister, who was ten weeks old, being held in the air by her proud mother. It was a scene out of *The Sound of Music*.

First realization: Not everyone is crazy about investing in photography—How much is too much to pay for any product or service?

As the mall started waking up Thursday morning, the public started checking out the different home show displays. "Wow! That's a big picture!" a prospective client mentioned. "Isn't it a beautiful story?" I volunteered. "How much does a big picture like that run?" He asked. "That size is X dollars." I replied. "X dollars?!" he exclaimed, "For a *picture?* Are you crazy?" As my first potential customer walked away incensed, I was speechless, hurt, and not looking forward to spending the next four days at this show. Ouch!

Oh no, here came another person, walking up to my pride and joy print. "Good morning," I offered, "How are you today?" They took in my print. "Just fine... Wow! That's a huge picture... How much is it?" With a deep breath, I apologetically said, "That size is X dollars." Gulp!

"That print is so beautiful and so worth the price! And what's that canvas texture? I love it!"

Now *this* person has taste and sees good value! I felt like Sally Fields at the Oscars... "You *do* like me, you really *do* like me!"

During the course of the show, I learned a lot from the general public. I learned, once again, that not everyone saw the artistic value of what I was trying to create... And you know, that's okay! You can't take it personally, like I did with that first person Thursday morning.

Realization #2: So, some of the public are willing to pay "top dollar" for my photography and some are not. Are there any common characteristics of the people that do see value in my work? As I gained my courage throughout the weekend, I started asking more questions. "What is it you like about this portrait? Why do you prefer the *Sound of Music* image over the "in-studio" photograph?

By the time we packed up everything Sunday night and headed home, I had my second revelation: prospective clients that saw value in my work were drawn to the images that were unique and different. The typical "in-studio" portrait was just that– typical!

As the months and years have gone by, I have studied the characteristics of our "perfect client." What do they have in common? Are they all left handed, 5'7", or former school teachers?

I've already given you a couple special characteristics: One, they're looking for something different and unique. Two, they view photography as an art form and see value in it. And three, they enjoy keeping in touch with our studio and appreciate that we maintain the relationship with them. These are just three in an ongoing list of the common characteristics that are contained in our "perfect client profile." This will be discussed in depth in a future chapter "In Search of the Perfect Client."

Consistency– Providing a quality experience

There have been countless books written about having a good first impression.

The first time you work with a client is in some ways the easy part. Making that experience consistent each time is the hard part of any business.

As I mentioned before, while growing up I sold a lot of stuff to my neighbors for various fund raising projects. Being the little entrepreneur of the neighborhood gave me many opportunities for other employment like mowing lawns. It didn't take much time to figure out that if I didn't do a good job every time, the kid two streets down would end up mowing instead of me. I also learned that when I said

I'd be there on Tuesday, I'd better be there on Tuesday! My neighbor three doors down taught me this lesson. I normally mowed her lawn on Thursdays. One week "something" came up and I didn't show up until Saturday morning. She was not happy. In fact, she was furious. I apologized, but it didn't seem to matter much. In my 13-year-old brain I was thinking, "What's the big deal? I was only two days late!" What I didn't know was that she had scheduled a party for Friday night and had assumed the yard was going to be in perfect shape. Oops! It was a hard lesson to learn, but I still live by it today.

When a client asks me, "When will my portraits be ready," instead of saying two to three weeks, I ask, "Is there a specific day when you need them by?" Portraits are the type of product that are always being used as gifts for birthdays, anniversaries, and lots of special occasions.

Being consistent on delivery times is the back bone of our studio, especially with all of the repeat clients we have. The business that can achieve this consistency is light years ahead of their competition.

I think restaurants probably have it the hardest when it comes to consistency. How many times have you gone to a restaurant expecting the great service and fantastic food quality you received the last time you visited, and were disappointed? It comes down to one premise— The more consistent your product and service is, the better chance you have of repeat clientele. It's hard building a relationship with anyone in just a single visit. Consistency is the essence of what relationship marketing is all about!

Asking Questions

The more questions you ask, the more you care, and the more your clients feel you care. I can't remember who taught me that valuable lesson or when I learned it, but it's at the heart of relationship marketing.

"Hi, Mrs. Stats, have you ever run out of Christmas wrapping paper on Christmas Eve?... Guess what I'm selling this time for our band!" Or, "How's your new kitten doing? I bet he's getting big!" The more questions you ask, the more you show you care. "Mrs. Adams, how short would you like your lawn this week? If I cut it too short, it might turn brown faster... What do you think?" Once again, the more you ask, the more you show you care. It seems pretty simple, doesn't it, but how many businesses really ask for exactly what the customer's needs are?

I attribute a large part of our studio's success today to just plain asking questions of my clients. How am I able to create images without asking what they're looking for? "Do you see the portrait being formal or casual, color or black and white, sharp or soft? What kind of feeling or mood did you have in mind? Who's going to be in the portrait? Is there a certain location where you would like the portrait taken?" These are all things that I need to know before I can even start the creation process. I've found over the years that the type of prospective client that's not willing to go through this process prior to the portrait session is probably not my type of client. Chances are, they're the type I met in our first mall show that was disgusted at paying X dollars "for a picture!"

The beauty of having this type of consultation prior to a portrait session, building a house, or having plastic surgery done, is that the client, customer, or patient has input into the process and also knows what he or she is getting into. One of my favorite television show openings starts out with the plastic surgeon asking his patient, "Tell me what you don't like about yourself."

The more questions you ask, the more you care. My "perfect client" thrives in this consultation environment. Many times I hear, "The other studios I called never asked me a single question– they just told me about their monthly special and wanted to make an appointment. They didn't seem to *care* about what I wanted!"

When I hear this, it just reinforces once again– The more questions you ask, the more you demonstrate care for your customer or client, further exploiting the weaknesses of your competitors who often do not demonstrate this level of caring. Taking the time and energy to ask your client or customer costs you nothing but it does give you the opportunity to gain their confidence, which is a great way to start any type of relationship.

2

WHAT IS RELATIONSHIP MARKETING?

To really get a good idea of relationship marketing, I think we have to talk a little bit about other forms of marketing, This is important because relationship marketing isn't something you can do the minute you open your doors.

To have relationships with clients, you need to have clients first, which is not a concept Sue and I learned when we first opened. Reading books such as <u>How to Win Customers and Keep them for Life</u>, by Michael LeBoeuf, <u>Customers for Life</u>, by Carl Sewell, and <u>Guerilla Marketing</u>, by Jay Conrad Levinson, gave us a good start.

I'd have to say it was really those three books that taught us about the different forms of marketing. I realize there are a lot of different theories out there on various forms of marketing, but what I've come up with for our purposes in this book are four distinct types of marketing.

Universal Marketing

The first type of marketing that we began using when we initially opened is what we call universal marketing. It's trying to get your name out to the public; everywhere!

Some of the earlier forms of this were having a phone book cover salesman come in and sell us space on one of those plastic phone book covers. (Of course, the Yellow Pages themselves are a form of universal marketing.) What about those coupons on the back of the receipts at grocery stores? We did that, too. With every salesman that came in the door, we fell victim. We did have some business prior to opening the store, but now that we were full-time in our own studio, we needed to beef up our marketing efforts by letting people know where we were. So we purchased ads in the local newspapers and did whatever we could to have people notice us and our new studio.

That's universal marketing, and it's probably the most costly of all the marketing forms, because you're reaching out to pretty much everybody. Sue used to have an analogy for universal marketing. She pictured it as standing on top of the Seattle Space Needle, throwing one dollar bills into the air with our studio name stamped on them, in hopes that someone would find one (maybe). They'd look at that one-dollar bill, see our name, and hopefully remember us and what we do when they needed our services someday.

It's a very inefficient and expensive way of getting your name out there because there's no real target—you're just throwing it out to everybody.

This brings us to the next type of marketing that we started doing, and that was more targeted marketing.

Targeted Marketing

That was the second form of marketing that we pursued. We found it to be a lot more effective, and a lot more cost-effective, too. We were marketing to less people now, but marketing to people who were going to need our service probably within a year's time.

We started targeting high school seniors through direct mail, using very accessible mailing lists in which we could get all the names and addresses for seniors in specific zip code areas. For example, high school senior portraits have become very popular, and usually the kids are going to have them done the summer before they graduate, or in our case in Seattle, they often wait until the springtime before they graduate to do their senior portraits. It's what we call an "immediate need" product. The majority of seniors need to have their portraits done during their senior year, so there's a good chance they are going to be in need of our product. Whether they choose us or not, that's another thing.

It's the same principle with wedding photography: We also targeted brides by going to bridal fairs, creating a booth, and letting people know about us and our incredible photography. A bride's going to a bridal fair to look for cake people, DJ's, and everything else for her wedding, so we found it very effective to be at a location where there were hundreds of brides looking for vendors like us.

Taking targeted marketing to the next level is something that I'm always looking for in my business. A great example of that is a direct mail piece that we created and sent to prospective clients that have lake front homes. The Seattle area has many lakes and as you can imagine the homes and property values are huge. Many of my clients live in these homes. After leaving one of these residences I started thinking, how nice it would be to get all of these specific addresses of people that live on that particular lake. How could I do that? I sought out a realtor friend's expertise who had access through title companies to obtain addresses in specific neighborhoods. I wondered if it would be possible to just get only the addresses of homes with lake front property and sure enough, those were available. I requested the names and addresses of 5 different lakes in the area. Rather than just creating any kind of marketing piece that features various types of family portraits in various locations I decided to produce a card that had images that pertained exclusively to lake front property, with images of families sitting on their dock or with their boat. You get the picture (no pun intended). And now when the prospective client receives one of our mailings they can truly relate to the message of having portraits taken right in their own backyard, in this case a beautiful lake. The results for this type of highly targeted marketing have been impressive. And as I write this book I'm looking for other opportunities to do the same with such things as pilot associates, classic car groups, and Harley

Davidson dealerships. The potentiality is endless! In doing such targeted marketing, we realized the effectiveness of going directly to the variety of people in need of our product or service.

Win-win marketing

Another form of marketing that we've used successfully is what we call win-win marketing which will be explained in further detail in the chapter by the same name.

When you are a part of a community, it's very important that you give back to that community. I highly recommend anyone in business getting involved in some kind of service group: Kiwanis, Soroptomists, or in my case, Rotary, to give back time, energy, and money to their community.

We've donated to the new performing arts center as well as our annual Summer-time festival "Renton River Days" and frequently donate to charity auctions, events that are not overly expensive and would fit into a small business budget. I really like to spend my marketing dollars on these kinds of things. Granted, it's somewhat like universal marketing: You're getting your name out there to a lot of people, and there's not a direct result or measurement of sales that you can immediately attribute to it. But it's the type of marketing that consistently gets your name out there in your community. Also you're perceived not just as somebody who's taking away from the community, but somebody who's giving back. I think that is very important. It is the right thing to do, and once again, part of being a viable member of the community.

Relationship marketing

So, finally, let's get into the whole concept of relationship marketing and what exactly it is.

The more years I've been in business, the more it's become clear that this is definitely where I want to spend the majority of dollars, time, and energy when it comes to marketing my studio. I'm fortunate because I've had a wonderful career since 1982, and have fantastic clients whose families have grown up along with my studio. One of the things that I most enjoy about my business is being able to be considered somebody's "family photographer." In some cases, I'll see a client once every year, and in some cases it might be ten or fifteen years before I see them again. One particular client comes to mind.

One story I would like to share with you is a couple I worked with some 15 years ago. They loved their wedding images. In fact, they had purchased a nice canvas wall portrait of an engagement image to display at their wedding. After their wedding, when they saw the photographs and we designed an album, they also purchased a nice 30x40 inch canvas portrait from one of their wedding images. They were extremely happy with what I created. This experience gave me the opportunity to develop the initial relationship and happened to be about the time we began collecting information for our databases. The goal was to acquire and track the names of our clients in hopes of having them come back when they had kids and when they had further photography needs. So every time I sent a Christmas card or sent out a newsletter, I would see this couple's name on the list.

I always wonder why some people decide to come back to you on a more frequent basis and why some people don't. That's something that always intrigues me. Well, fifteen years went by, and about two or three weeks after 9/11, I got a phone call from this bride of fifteen years ago, and the first thing out of her mouth was, "Bruce, I know I haven't talked to you in a long time, but I'm so sorry about Sue." At that point, Sue had passed away about seven years prior, and right then it really hit me that even though I hadn't talked to or seen this particular client in fifteen years, they had been in touch with me and the studio through our newsletters and various marketing pieces. That's when it became crystal clear how important relationship marketing really is.

I asked this client, "Why have you decided to call me now?" She replied, "Well, we just had our fourth child, and he's now three years old. My husband also started his own business...we've been kind of busy the last fifteen years! But we knew when our last child was to an age where he would cooperate, we would want to really invest in a nice portrait created by you."

For 15 years these clients had been receiving my information and it eventually led them back to me. This one incident reinforced the concept of relationship marketing and its importance to my business! Even though I hadn't heard from them in 15 years of sending newsletters and cards, they relentlessly and consistently heard from me, elements that helped build the relationship. It's almost like having a person next to you lightly tapping on your shoulder, always reminding you that, "Hey, I'm still here! I haven't gone away! And whenever you need me again, I'm here for you." Building relationships does not happen overnight and Relationship Marketing is not an instant gratification type of thinking. But, it will keep your clients coming back, even after a decade and a half.

Now, there's a way of overdoing it, and I think there's a balance you have to try and find. But what I find amazing, especially in my profession, is that often I will start photographing my clients as a one-year-old baby, and fifteen, sixteen, or seventeen years later, I'm doing their senior portraits, and then their weddings, and then their babies… That to me is the power of what relationship marketing is all about. It's keeping in touch; it's just laying low and being there on the sidelines. And when they do have a need, they're not going to forget you; they're going to call you and make sure you're the person that's going to be servicing them again. For the most part, these are people we've worked with for a long time; they're definitely part of our 'family' and we're a part of theirs.

So how do you get started with relationship marketing? Well, first of all you need some clients to have a relationship with. My recommendation is that you get a really good database program of some kind, one that's going to have names, addresses, phone numbers, and email addresses, as well as maybe an area for some notes about your clients: what their likes and dislikes are, maybe even their anniversary date or their kids' birthdays. Purchasing and developing an extremely solid database along with getting all the information entered, is the foundation of relationship marketing.

For years, once we finished with a client, we just placed their file in a box and that was it. That was before we started using computers and before we even knew what a database was. Now I look at our database as truly the lifeblood of my business. Being able to keep in touch with our clients is what has kept the studio going strong through a few recessions. So purchasing a user-friendly program, and developing your client database is the first thing I would highly recommend.

My second recommendation is to send out a letter to existing clients in your database. Let them know that you're goal is to try and keep in touch with them a little better. We do this with a newsletter. It's a wonderful way to let people know what's going on. As I mention in the upcoming chapter on newsletters, try not to commercialize it too much, but try to personalize it as much as you can. That's what people are going to respond to the best, rather than advertising a special offer that month, or something of that nature. It's more about what's new in your business. Do you have any new employees? If you do, feature them. In the case of my own kids, letting my clients see their progress has been fun: graduating from Kindergarten, high school, or, more recently, from college.

In the case of losing Sue back in 1996, the outpouring of love and support we received was truly amazing. Such support is expected from friends and family, but not from clients. This was not the case for us. As Sue's cancer escalated and became a terminal situation, news circulated quickly throughout the community. We were instantly inundated with phone calls and walk-ins, wanting to know Sue's status. I was gone most of the time at the hospital and then later at home. It became almost impossible for my employees to handle all of the outpouring and do the day to day studio tasks as well. So, we finally got to a point where we started having a daily "Sue update" that we created on our phone message machine. At the time, it could handle up to 200 calls at one time. It was unbelievable to be there in the studio when the phone started ringing off the hook at 5:00pm every evening for people to find out what Sue's status was in the final weeks and days. When she did pass away, we immediately sent out a card to let people know, and at that point, because of the outpouring that we received from the masses, the kids & I decided to do a memorial service in her name. 750 people attended this celebration of her life.

With all the marketing aside, I marvel at how many lives Sue had touched through the business. And when everyone learned that she had cancer and things were looking grim, it was astonishing how we were able to keep in touch with a lot of people over that time. It really shows you how one person can touch so many people's lives.

So, when beginning relationship marketing, those first two steps are important: developing your client database and then letting your clients know that you are going to be keeping in touch with them, keeping them up-to-date as to what's going on. Once again you're basically just tapping them on the shoulder from time to time to remind them that you're always there for them.

Next, with whatever business you have, it's really important to sit down, start planning, and map out a schedule for implementation. When we first started doing the newsletters, we did it sporadically. When we found our stride and perfected our format, we sent them out every quarter or so. Now we're at the point where we're at about every six months with this particular newsletter. With the advent of Email and broadcast Emails, we've been able to come up with a program we're very happy with. So for us, it has become more of an E-newsletter now, and we're able to do things more last-minute. But having a plan of action and mapping out when you're going to send out various items is important.

Along those same lines, maybe you have different levels of clients. In this chapter we're going to talk about our Premier Portrait Club, which includes my major stockholders, the clients who have used me many times. You've probably heard of the 80/20 rule, where 20% of your clients make up 80% of your sales, and this is definitely the case with our Premier Portrait Club. These are the people we want to keep in touch with more. And so, when you're mapping out a marketing calendar for the year, take this into account, that the people who are bringing you the most revenue are probably the ones you want to keep in touch with more than the rest of your clients.

Some of the beauty of relationship marketing is that when your existing clients do return, it's not like you have to re-educate them as to how your business works. In our case, we show our images via projection verses the old-fashioned paper proof method. The first time doing this does take some education. We have what we call consultations, in which clients come to the studio and we discuss such things as where the portrait is going to be taken, what they like to do as a family, where they see the portrait hanging in their home, clothing to be worn, and how we're going to try to color harmonize the clothing and the setting with the room in which it's going to be hanging. We also go over the way they're going to see their images initially, via projection. It's so much easier to work with somebody who's already been through the process and is well educated on what looks good in a portrait, how to dress, and how they're going to see their images. It just takes a lot less time, energy, and money to educate those people. So that's one of the beauties of working with clients that you have worked with in the past instead of always trying to beat the brush for new ones. Unfortunately, I think what happens with a lot of businesses is that they didn't create the product or service the client had expected. They didn't meet or exceed expectations as we try to do everyday, and so they're constantly going after new blood. Not getting existing clients to come back in any business can be very frustrating. I remember a principle I learned from one of the books by Carl Sewell titled Customers for Life mentioned earlier: It takes ten times as much time, energy, and money to attract new clients as it does to keep the old clients around and keep them happy.

Even if you do a good job or even a great job the first time, there's no guarantee clients are going to come back. You need to be there to remind them how great of a job you did and that they had an incredible experience. You will still be there anytime they want you. And, in most cases, when it comes to relationship marketing or any kind of marketing, it's just doing it or implementing the concept. This is probably one of the most frustrating but also most satisfying aspects for me as a teacher and educator today. I'm basically preaching the same ideas that Sue and I preached years ago. The marketing strategies that have worked for us in our studio are not earth shattering, but are effective if you put them into practice. Most seminar participants never actually implement the ideas they learn.

Step three is creating a calendar detailing when you're actually going to be sending these communications out and sticking to it. If you just have a few clients, you just send out a few newsletters. If you have a lot of clients, obviously it's going to take a little bit more money and time to make that happen, but I'll tell you, after seeing it work year after year, it's worth the effort. I can almost be guaranteed, once I send out an E-newsletter or one of our fancier newsletters, we're going to get a couple phone calls that day for people to sign up for one of our portrait safaris, which you will hear more about in "Creating the Experience", or just say, "You know, this is like the straw that broke the camel's back. We've been meaning to do this family portrait for years, and I've seen this newsletter for years, and it just kept reminding me that this is what we need to do."

So, what is relationship marketing? It's a form of marketing to your existing customers or clients that allows them to keep in touch with you on their terms. It's an organized, planned, constant subtle reminder that will pay back massive dividends throughout the life of your business.

In the next chapter I'm going to introduce you to various forms of relationship marketing. Although the system and strategies may be different, the end game is always the same: keeping in touch and maintaining the valuable relationship you have with your clients or customers!

3

STARTING THE RELATIONSHIP AND CREATING THE EXPERIENCE

I believe two things are important in business: relationship marketing, what this book is all about, and *creating the experience* for your client, something they're going to remember you by. Creating that experience for your clients is something that separates you from your competition.

I learned this theory early on in life, and then, as I mentioned in the first chapter, in business. When we first started in 1982, one area that we saw a lot of potential for growth was high school senior portraits. Back when I had my own senior portraits in the early 1970's, it was just about going to a trailer and sitting down in front of the photographer for maybe 20 or 30 seconds, and click-click-click...next! The portrait was mainly used for the yearbook, but you had the opportunity to buy a package for 30 or 40 dollars that had enough photographs in it to last a lifetime, or so it seemed.

But in 1982, things were a little different. Senior portraits had evolved into multiple outfits, different clothing changes, and different sets. One of our biggest competitors at that time was advertising three outfits and an "unhurried" 20 minute session. Well, it might not sound like much by today's standards of senior portraits, but it's all kind of relevant to the time, compared to the 30-second session I had in the 70's. So we needed to find something that we could do that the competition wasn't willing to do, and we found that to be adding outdoor portraits to the session. And it wasn't that our competitors weren't *willing* to do that, it's just that they didn't *want* to do it. They were looking to do three sessions an hour in the camera room; they would do the outdoor portrait, but the outdoor portrait part of that session cost so much, that it really deterred people from wanting to do it. We found that this set us apart from other photographers: *we* were willing to go out into a park or maybe even to the home of the senior, and do some outdoor portraits, which was totally different, a completely different look than what was the norm at the time and thus giving us the competitive edge.

So when we moved our studio from a shopping center to our own building, we wanted to make sure the building had some opportunities for outdoor photography, one of the main reasons we selected the property we did. We have an acre out back that has a number of outdoor sets (like a little Universal Studios); we have an area that's like a gas station, where kids can bring their cars, and we do a lot of black and white, urban stuff there. We have gazebo areas, we have stucco archways, and even a waterfall. It's a pretty neat operation that usually evokes a "Wow!" with my client's first visit. It's part of the *experience* that we share when they're photographed at Hudson's.

But now, twenty-some years later, outdoor portraits have become the norm. So what we've tried to do is go to that *next* step to separate us from other studios, where we actually go on location to different areas where the kids hang out- it might be a skateboard park, a horse barn, or a sport court- and photograph them "doing their thing" in their natural habitat! It might be a lake where they're wakeboarding; it might even be going up into the mountains and getting shots of them skiing or snowboarding. And so, once again, we're trying to find certain things where we're able to create an *experience* for our clients that are unique and different than what our competition has.

One of my favorite books on this subject was written many years ago: How to Win Customers and Keep them for Life by Michael

LeBoeuf. The author talks about how to win customers, creating an experience that is different and unique, and drawing certain types of clientele to you because of that experience.

Over the years, we've analyzed the demographics of the type of person we consider to be our perfect client, the characteristics of what they like, and hopefully what has attracted them to us. And at the top of the list is that they're looking for something different, something more artistic. For example, earlier in our career, back in the 1980's, black and white photography was not all that popular, We offered it and provided our "perfect" clients something other studios weren't doing. More recently, we've been offering a product that looks more like a watercolor painting than a photograph, which is manipulated in Photoshop© and printed on watercolor paper. So we're always looking for something that looks a little different, because we've found that the type of client *we're* looking for, who really respects photography as art, is looking for something different. We at Hudson's are always on the lookout for ways of creating new products and new experiences for our clients that will attract them to our studio.

Another thing we do to create an experience for our clients is location work, especially with family portraits. In a traditional family-type portrait, you go to a studio, the photographer pulls down a background, poses the family, and that's pretty much it. But back in the late 1970's there were quite a few photographers, especially here in the Northwest, who started doing portraits outside, instead of the traditional studio-type background. I studied with many of those photographers early in my career and learned posing and lighting techniques that work well outdoors.

What we now try to do is to incorporate as much of the family's personality as possible into that image. Maybe they're farmers in the middle of the state; if so, we want to try and incorporate the fields and then combines into their portrait. Or over on the western side of the state, they might be into boating, and so we want to try and utilize that into their image. The more we personalize their portrait, the more they enjoy it, and the more it heightens the whole family portrait experience.

Another thing we do to try to create an exceptional experience for our clients is to offer what we call Portrait Safaris. With these Portrait Safaris, we try to not just provide a photo shoot, but make it an event using different locations, different times of the year, and so forth. Locally, when the leaves turn, we book a full Saturday and a full Sunday, going out to a park where there's a lot of maple trees changing color, and make it a very special event called Portrait in the Leaves. Adding to that experience, we also bring homemade chili, hot spiced cider, pumpkin cookies, those kinds of things. When the clients arrive for their session, they can spend some time at our picnic table and have something to snack on before or after their session, making it an even more fun experience for them.

Every August we do a Portrait Safari at Cannon Beach, Oregon, which I think is probably one of the most beautiful beaches in the world. Instead of just having a beach with sand, you have these beautiful rock monoliths sticking out of the ocean as part of the background. Almost every evening at 5:00 p.m., even in the summer time, a wonderful fog rolls in giving you this incredible soft defused light that is spectacular for portraits. Many of my clients plan their family vacations at Cannon Beach around our August dates. To me, it's the ultimate compliment!

As we do with Portraits in the Leaves, we bring goodies to the beach to enjoy after their session. It's fun to share a bottle of wine with clients as the sun sets and the night begins. My passion for creating something special for my clients doesn't just lie behind the camera, but includes the total experience of the event. The Portrait Safari concept, which started locally, has now expanded to Napa, Maui, and even Tuscany! I found over the years the further the distance, the more exotic the location, the better the experience for my client, That's just one of those things we do to separate ourselves from other photographers and studios by creating an experience that is memorable and something that they can tell *their* friends about.

Another facet of creating the experience is the way our clients see their images (we used to call them proofs). The traditional method of presenting images had always been to make a set of 4x5 or 5x5 proofs. The client picks them up, takes them home, and decides what they want to purchase. For many years, we've projected their images by screening a slide show set to music, followed by a more detailed look at each image, often using side-by-side comparisons of similar photographs so clients can decide which they like best. To finalize the image, often times I'll take the projector to their home, projecting right onto the wall on which they're going to be hanging that portrait. This way they can see *exactly* what the image looks like before we take the time and energy to actually create the final portrait. It's almost like trying on a tailor-made suit, prior to the suit being made. It is a brilliant way for my clients to visualize exactly what the portrait is going to look like on their wall. It takes *all* the guess work out of the decision making process. Many clients ask if there's any additional cost for this service. I say, "No, this is just all part of the experience we're trying to provide for you."

Ivar's Acres of Clams

Does relationship marketing and creating the experience just pertain to higher-end products and services? To me the answer is no. I want to share a Seattle landmark that understands that relationships start the first time you walk in their doors!

When I travel, it's always fun to visit local hangouts. Let's take burgers as an example: In Seattle we have *Dick's Drive-In*, in Los Angeles they have *In and Out Burger*, and in Kansas City they have *Town Topic*. Every city has certain types of restaurants that have been around forever, and they're very entrenched in the culture of that particular city. In Seattle, which is known for seafood, we have *Ivar's Acres of Clams*.

Ivar Haglund sang his inspiration repeatedly on the radio, from *The Old Settler*:

THE RELATIONOGRAPHER

No longer a slave to ambition
I laugh at the world and its shams
As I survey my happy condition
Surrounded by acres of clams.

He began this Northwest tradition in 1938 and was determined that the restaurant be built around public awe and admiration. His warm, albeit eccentric, personality has caught Seattle's attention since their first introduction. In 1940, Ivar and his seal, Patsy, made their way to Frederick & Nelson's department store to visit Santa Claus, causing quite a stir. When a railroad car filled with syrup began to leak onto the roads outside Ivars restaurant, there was a display of fun when Ivar could be seen in the middle of the puddle of syrup, waders and all, pouring the syrup over his restaurants pancakes exclaiming, "Eat at Ivar's, we don't skimp on the syrup."[1] He was an amazing man who always gave back to the community. He agreed to sponsor a fireworks festival in 1964 that was about to be cancelled unless someone came forward to sponsor the event. He decided to use the opportunity as a way to thank his customers and give back to the community that helped make his restaurants so successful. The event has been going on ever since. People still come to enjoy the *Forth of Jul-Ivars* fireworks on Elliot Bay. Ivars also encourages its local chain restaurants to give donations, such as gift certificates in silent auctions, or 30-50 gallons of chowder to cancer walks at local high schools. They try and donate to as many good causes as they can!

Ivar himself has been gone for a number of years, but that spirit and attitude are still a part of the Ivar's tradition. Today, the business has evolved into three main restaurants and over twenty smaller seafood bars. One of those smaller establishments is very close to my studio. This particular restaurant used to be lower-middle in the company ranks, but now they are 5th out of 25 stores! They got a new manager several years ago, and it skyrocketed. How did they do it?

I hadn't been in there in quite a while because the quality of the food and service had deteriorated, but I thought I'd give it another try and was surprised to find it was a different place. As I ordered my food, instead of giving me a number, they asked for my name, which I gave and sat down. What I witnessed was remarkable. As every person came into that restaurant, the person behind the register (and it happened to be the manager or the assistant manager) knew them by their first name. Later I found out that most other Ivars' stores only know about 100 names, but the crew at the store near the studio have made it a point to know 700-800. They train their employees to know the customer's name through certain steps. Every time they take something to the customer, they use that name. The manager believed that the more times you use a person's name, the easier it is to remember in the long term. I was amazed! These customers were being treated as though they were at a five-star restaurant they frequented all the time. People respond to that positively because of personal recognition and attention.

It wasn't that all these people were coming there just for the food; they were coming there because they were known and they were recognized. I believe that's a very valuable thing when it comes to relationship marketing: the service or business instills the kind of feeling in the customer that he or she is somebody whose patronage is most appreciated. Just the simple thing of knowing their name when you see them instills that appreciation. And it's not just, once again, a big five-star hotel or four-star restaurant, it can happen at a fast food place like *Ivar's Acres of Clams*.

Another thing I noticed was that this particular Ivar's had a new product on the menu. Growing up in Seattle and visiting Ivar's for as long as I can remember, I've always enjoyed the world-famous clam chowder they're known for. One of the things I like about Ivar's is that you have a choice: you can have the white chowder, which is more traditional, or you can have the red chowder, which is called 'Manhattan' style. But on this day they had a third chowder that used smoked salmon. I ordered some, and it was very tasty. I talked to the manager about that, too, and his response was, "Well, you know we have a lot of Muslim customers who come in, and Muslims can't order the chowder, because of the pork [bacon] in it, so we developed this smoked salmon chowder especially for those customers." And I thought, *"how smart is that"?* When you get to know your customers and build a relationship with them, you'll find out what they like and what they don't like. In this case, it had to do with taste and religion, so this particular Ivar's pioneered a new smoked salmon chowder just for a certain customer base, and it became so popular that they're now doing it in all the Ivar's restaurants.

Hotel Monaco
Creating the experience and making it memorable.

I've stayed in hundreds of hotels over the years, and I'm sure you have too. Hotels have such a great opportunity to provide a memorable experience for their guests. Many hotels hit that on the mark, and unfortunately most hotels completely miss it. I want to tell you about a story of the Hotel Monaco. It's actually a Kipton property and they have hotels all over the world. Oddly enough, one of my favorite hotels in Seattle, and I do like to be tourist in Seattle from time to time, is Hotel Monaco. It's a very warm, luscious, award winning hotel. In fact, some of their recent awards have been one of the top 500 hotels in the world, with *Travel and Leisure* magazine; the top hotels price range from $250-$400 a night in the United States. It also received the gold list award and the world's hippest hotel, 2004 *In Style* magazine.

What makes the Hotel Monaco so special you ask, and how do they create such a neat experience for their guests? Well, it's a fun atmosphere. The architecture is very warm and inviting and has a Monaco, 1920's art deco feel, with a motto expressing "indulge your senses." You can get rooms at the hotel Monaco sometimes for under $200 which still includes complimentary services. Some of these complimentary things range from high speed internet throughout the hotel (that's pretty standard for an upscale hotel), to complimentary

Starbucks coffee service, that proves to be a **must** in Seattle. They also take delivering newspapers one step further, not only do they give you a complimentary newspaper, but one of your choice. They also have a complimentary social evening called "an hour of indulgence" by the fireplace. On Tuesday and Thursday nights you can have chair massages and something unique on Wednesdays and Saturdays is a fortune teller.

Every hotel tells a story, and Hotel Monaco's story is of animals. From their dolphin murals and Guppy Love, they have special events and programs that cater to animal societies. It is a celebration of all earth's creatures. If you don't bring a pet, one will actually be assigned to you: a complimentary goldfish. They call it the original Guppy Love. I recently was there on Valentine's Day with Terri and we decided to ask for 2 goldfish. They came in their own private bowls, so we combined them so they could enjoy Valentines Day as well! Every turn they are providing a neat experience, I suggest that if you're ever in Seattle, check out the Hotel Monaco. If you get our Goldfish, Roger or Sadie please tell them we said HI!

Finally, in getting to know your customers and their needs, you start developing a relationship that's innovative. With Ivars, it's being recognized as you walk in the door and having products created especially for your customers. At the Hotel Monaco, it is doing something totally unique to create a memorable experience that will set you apart from your competition and attract a level of client/customer that will keep coming back. May it be photography, staying at a world class hotel or fish and chips, you can bet if you create a memorable experience, you're guaranteed to have a loyal patron for life!

---

[1] *Ivar's Timeline*, http://www.ivars.net, 2006.

4

IN SEARCH OF THE PERFECT CLIENT...
Why is relationship marketing so effective?

I've always noticed that our very best clients all have similar personalities, and many of the same characteristics. What are some of these matching characteristics of your clients or customers? Are they all left-handed, non smokers, democrats, or republicans? Do they all love to fish or hunt, scrapbook and drive Mercedes? Have you ever noticed that it's much easier to work with some clients or customers than it is with others? Why is that? Some have certain characteristics that just gel with you, your service, and product. Sue and I had this revelation when Phantom of the Opera was popular and playing in Vancouver B.C. We actually had three wedding clients that proposed at the Phantom of the Opera. We were thinking, "Wow, is that a coincidence or what?" So we began analyzing who our best clients/ perfect clients were. Over the years we've come up with a list of these patterns and characteristics common to all our perfect clients. Let's take a closer look to give you a little flavor as to who our perfect clients are and how similar they are to one another. Better yet, you'll also see why relationship marketing is so effective.

Eccentric
Nearly all our clients are eccentric. "Eccentric" can have different meanings, so to help clarify I'll share one of my favorite stories of a

THE RELATIONOGRAPHER

Japanese gentleman that got married in the Seattle area. We got the call just three weeks before the wedding, which is pretty rare, because we're normally booked ten to eighteen months before a wedding. The call came from a wedding planner who had sent a lot of clients our way over the years and she asked, "Are you available in three weeks?" Sue and I looked at each other thinking that's pretty flaky...what kind of client would wait to hire a photographer for their wedding until the last possible minute? We were available and decided to book the wedding. Price was not an issue with this client, but we did require that we meet with them at least once before the wedding to discuss their photography needs, get to know them a little and start building a relationship. They cancelled a few appointments, but the Friday before the wedding, at about 4:30pm, a black stretch limousine, rolled into the studio parking lot. Upon exiting the limo I noticed they were carrying bags from McDonalds! This seemed a little strange. I was finishing up with a client in the studio so Sue took them downstairs to our projection room and showed them the slide show and started the all important "bonding process" by asking them what they're looking for in their wedding photography. I came in twenty minutes later and immediately we became good friends. Thanks to Sue's ability to instantly relate to anyone, they had invited us to Japan to photograph their wedding in Japan which would take place in a couple months. Very eccentric, very spontaneous! Eccentric clients tend to think in the moment and be extremely impulsive. Photography is a very emotional product and service. It can create instant emotions. You're familiar with the phrase, "A picture is worth a thousand words." Well, an image can also evoke a thousand feelings and emotions as well. I learned this early on in my career. Remember our first mall display in the first chapter, where I received two very different opinions with in minutes? Our new found eccentric friends and clients were exhibiting very normal behavior for them—being impulsive—which ended up being a fantastic opportunity for Sue and me to travel to Japan!

So what are some other characteristics similar to our perfect clients?

Professional or Self Employed

I deal with a lot of dentists, doctors, and business owners. I would call my clients very much "self-made people," more new money than the traditional old money types. They are extremely hard working and love what they do—every day.

Romantic

These perfect people tend to be romantic. This ties in with the original characteristic Sue and I had recognized many years ago with the Phantom of the Opera. Time and again I've heard countless stories from my wedding clients about how they met and their first impressions of each other. It's always fun to listen to their stories and eventually ask how they were proposed to. While I have been building relationships with my clients I have heard lots of phantom-like stories. Besides the Phantom of the Opera, one of my favorites was the client that put a ring in an oyster shell and set it in a tide pool at the ocean (you'll hear the whole story in an up coming chapter). It's a type of characteristic that you wouldn't think would be tied into the perfect client. But for us, since the product of photography has such an emotional appeal which evokes a lot of feelings, you can see how it is related. After I show a slide show at our first meeting, I ask our clients what images they liked and disliked. Undoubtedly the images they are drawn to tend to be the ones more romantic in nature. Some examples would be the groom kissing the bride on the neck or the two of them looking at each other in an intimate way. Most of the guys wouldn't admit that, especially in front of their groomsman and buddies, but in the presence of their fiancé and me, they tend to admit they do like the romantic stuff. My perfect client is also drawn to the spontaneity we encourage during a session instead of merely being "posed." This leads to their attraction of the next characteristic--- something different.

Looking for Something Different

The "same old-same old" isn't what my clients are searching for.

THE RELATIONOGRAPHER

They are unique individuals and tend to seek out something different, especially in photography. I'm not sure that black and white is all that new today, but back in the 1980's and early 1990's, we did do a lot of black and white when most other studios were not offering that option. I feel we attracted new clients that are still here with us today simple because we offered this service and provided something outside the ordinary.

Quality

Our clients tend to buy top-of-the-line products. Typically they are willing to spend the extra dollars to get the top of the line portrait, which is photographic paper bonded to canvas. It tends to make our portraits look more like a painting. This level of quality is demonstrated consistently through their lifestyle. They don't drive the entry model car, but the mid- to higher-end vehicle. You can also tell by their jewelry and the homes they live in. They enjoy the finer things in life and they invest in them. These clients also prefer products that clearly demonstrate value. If they are going to invest in top-of-the-line services and products, they expect them to last a long time. We can support this expectation through the type of photographic paper we use, which is Fuji paper, which lasts 5 times as long as other photographic paper out there in the market. This is a selling point I stress to my clients. I let them know that these prints are not going to fade or go away. They have an 80 year longevity! That increases the value of my product from my client's perspective.

Views Photography as Art

Some people don't recognize photography as an art form. My perfect clients do. Art to them includes many styles and mediums. They display my work proudly in their homes. They're also proud to display images of their family. It's a form of art that just happens to contain them as the subject.

34

IN SEARCH OF THE PERFECT CLIENT...

Views my Work as an Investment

It's always hard to put a price tag on art. As I mentioned earlier, my first mall display was a real eye opener. If you recall, I would have one person come up, comment on how much they loved the prints, ask how much they cost and then tell me it's too expensive and not worth the money! In contrast, the next individual I talked to loved the prints and felt they had great value.

As my business has evolved over time, so have my prices. I am not considered an inexpensive photographer. But my clients do see me as a great investment. They're not only investing in my work as an art piece but also as an heirloom of the family for generations to come.

Family Values

Our perfect clients value their family over anything else. I think that's one reason why my perfect clients invest a lot in family portraits.

Custom-made

They also like customized products. So when I work with these prefect clients, we talk about customizing their portraits to fit a certain space in their home. Or we can customize a portrait by using wardrobe or setting color to capture the mood and feeling for where the portrait is going to be hung. This aspect of "custom made" is really important: they are always looking for something different! They don't want the "same old, same old," but something unique.

Organization and Follow-up

When a potential client calls us and wants information about our services, we do our best to send that information immediately. Here is a great story that illustrates my point. I got a call from a woman who just had a new baby and wanted to update her portrait. In most cases, potential clients on the phone will call and ask, "How much are your 8x10s?" It's very rare when they say, "I want to update my 30x40 inch canvas portrait." But this was one of those cases where they had already invested in portraiture while living in California, and that's what they wanted up here in Seattle. She was shopping around and basically just wanted information. She seemed very business like and very to the point. I got the impression that she did not want me to sell her anything, but just send her information. "If I like what I see, I'll call you back." I wanted to be able to fulfill her request in a timely manner and make a strong impression. Even though the town she was in was only 20-30 minutes from the studio, I opted to send it UPS Ground instead of US Mail, so the information would get there over night. I assembled a package which included our video brochure (a brief infomercial), as well as pricing information and some collateral brochures for family portraits. About 2 weeks later I noticed that she was booked for a consultation to discuss her family portrait ideas. When I met her for the first time in the projection room, I thanked her for coming and asked, "What made you decide to choose us?" She replied, "Well, you're the only people that sent me anything and you did it over night! I was very impressed!" I had recognized during our initial conversation that she liked things to be expedited in a timely fashion and had a lot of respect for organization. Luckily, I was able to fulfill her needs and she became a life long client.

The final three client characteristics relate totally to relationship marketing and why it is so effective.

Love to Keep in Touch

My perfect clients love to keep in touch with us, and they enjoy when we keep in touch with them. This is an ongoing relationship that works especially well with newsletters and e-newsletters. We try to keep them informed, not just about the studio events, but also what is going on both in my life and the life of my family. As I mentioned in the newsletter chapter, my goal is always to personalize instead of commercialize. Many clients tell me they appreciate this initiative.

Enjoy Relationships

You can tell that my clients love to be involved with people and relationships. They're very committed to their children's schools, sports, and activities. They also have a lot of friends, they're active with people at church, and with many other organizations. They just enjoy having relationships. This is a big part of their lives. It's once again what fuels our reason to keep in touch with our clients. It's also something that gets them all jazzed up! They are a part of our life and we like to feel as though we are a part of theirs. It's all about relationships.

Rewarded for Loyalty

The last characteristic that I would like to share with you is our perfect clients reward and are rewarded for loyalty. We will be discussing this in a future chapter entitled, "Welcome to the Club", is our perfect clients enjoy being rewarded for their loyalty to a business. They like the fact that if they're going to be coming back time and time again, may it be Alaska Airlines, Border's Books, or their favorite coffee shop, loyalty has its rewards. So over the years, we've instituted our Premiere Portrait Club, which rewards our very best and thanks them for their loyalty and allows us to continue our relationship over the years.

So who is the Perfect Client?

I think it's important in any kind of business, whether retail or service, for you to be absolutely certain, you really know your target market is and the demographics of your prospective clients. This gives you a basis for the type of customer or client that you want to attract. It's important to recognize where they come from and what they like to do. There are a lot of creative ways to attract a client by providing an experience that is unique to them. In the case of our business, having the knowledge that a romantic style of photography attracts brides into my studio is key. You bet I'm going to display, either in my lobby or at wedding shows, images that will invoke those romantic tendencies. And I'll always be working to be more organized, especially when sensing clients who want information quickly, even if it takes overnight delivery!

So why is relationship marketing so powerful for our business? Once again, the three strongest characteristics my perfect client exhibits are a love of building relationships, enjoy the fact that we keep in touch, and appreciate being rewarded for their loyalty for the relationship we've built with them. Relationship marketing has been such an incredible tool in our business and I'm certain it has the same potential for yours. I encourage you to sit down and take the time to discover just who your perfect client really is. I've created a little worksheet to guide you though examples of who your perfect clients are and what their characteristics are. Enjoy the journey!

IN SEARCH OF THE PERFECT CLIENT...

Your *PERFECT* Clients

Name(s)—What made them *Perfect Clients?*

1)

2)

3)

4)

Common (threads) characteristics

1)

2)

3)

4)

5)

6)

7)

"Finding a balance in business and life... artistic fulfillment with financial rewards"

5

THE ART OF KEEPING IN TOUCH
Newsletters and E-Newsletters

Without a doubt, creating and mailing newsletters to our clients has been the best value for our marketing dollars. My clients love the fact that I keep in touch with them via the newsletter. It's amazing that when I bump into a client, say in a mall or grocery store, the first thing they mention is not how much they have enjoyed their portraits, but how they have enjoyed the newsletters.

Why is that? I think it comes down to the fact that we try to personalize and not commercialize it. My late wife Sue was a master at writing our newsletter. She had an incredible ability to write as though she was sitting across the table from you having coffee. This genuine and sincere approach makes our newsletter very entertaining to read. Today, I still try to write in the highly personal style in which Sue wrote.

Here's a quick overview of our <u>newsletter basics</u>.

1. Who do you send them to?

a) Our past clients—keeping in touch is what relationship marketing is all about.

b) Prospective clients that may have come in to inquire about our services, but opted not to work with us at that time.

c) Our vendors. I think it's good to have your suppliers informed of what you're up to. I see my vendors almost as silent partners in my business. It's always smart to keep your partners in the loop.

d) People in the community that you work with but aren't clients yet. This group includes people in my Rotary Club and the Chamber of Commerce. They might not need my services now, but when they do, I'll be the first on their mind!

e) Lastly, my personal friends and family. We all look forward to receiving cards during the holidays. Many families have started the tradition of letters outlining the past years events. It's a great way to keep in touch with your loved ones and the special people in your life.

2. When do you send your newsletters? When is it too much or too little?

You are the only one to judge that. The frequency of our newsletters is based on resources, time, and budget. How much time and energy can you spend producing and sending it out? Again, you and only you can answer that! How much of your marketing dollars are you willing to invest?

For us at *Hudson's Designer Portraits*, we try our best to send our newsletters every quarter. It's the perfect balance of keeping in touch and sticking with the marketing budget for my business.

Let's talk about timing for a moment. Some businesses have busy times, slow times, and times when they need to remind their clients and customers when to buy. At the studio, summer is always a great time to have family portraits outdoors. We send our newsletter out a couple months prior to summer. One of the feature stories will discuss having your portrait made during the summer months. I view the use of newsletters and keeping in touch as if each quarter year, we are standing beside our valuable clients or customers, and softly tapping them on the shoulder to remind them that we, their favorite photographer is still around and part of their life.

3. What goes in the newsletter?

Personalized, not commercialized, right?

We try to have the cover or opening page be a feature story. For us a feature story is something that's new, fresh, or special for the studio. We've used topics like "Dream Assignments" where we've traveled to Japan or Hawaii to photograph a wedding, or a "Seven-Generation" feature where we tell the story of a portrait session that highlights seven generations in two photographs. The first photograph was taken in 1915 and the 2nd photograph was my work. The 8 month old in the 1915 photograph was the great grandmother in the portrait I created. It was an amazing experience!

Other types of stories we include are, as Sue called them, anchor stories. They have the same theme each issue, but updated content. Here are some examples:

• "Client Corner":

This is where we feature clients that have special things happening in their life, such as expecting or having a baby, getting married, or receiving an award. How do we get the information? Many times our clients let us know by sending baby announcements, or it might even be something that we see in the newspaper.

• "Rappin' with Retouch"– What's that?!

Well, for many years we had a studio cat named Retouch, named for the photographic term. He was a very cool cat that our clients loved, so Sue and I decided that Retouch needed to have his own column in the newsletter! It was kind of 'life at the studio from a cat's perspective.' To say the least, it was a very popular column or anchor story in the newsletter. Years later, when Retouch went to kitty heaven, *(that Great Litter Box in the Sky?)* his story was, of course, a feature story in our next newsletter. It's hard to believe, but we received cards and even flowers in remembrance of Retouch.

• A Schedule of events

Over the years we've developed a concept that we call Portrait

Safaris, as mentioned in Creating the Experience. I like to offer my clients special locations for their portrait session during prime weather or top season conditions. The safaris can range from a park in the fall featuring beautiful leaves, to Napa wine country during the harvest and crush season, to beach portraits in Maui!

Many of these require some pre-planning, so we try to publish the schedule in each newsletter. It never hurts to let your customers know of upcoming special events, sometimes a year in advance. Planning and communication is key in relationship marketing.

• To round out the newsletter, on the back page we always have a featured portrait. It's always difficult chosing the featured portrait because of all my options. I usually look for something different, creative, and unique to tantalize my readers. One new idea will always spark even more ideas!

The content for your newsletter will of course vary depending on the type of business or service you have, but I can't stress enough the importance of personalizing it as much as possible. The majority of your clients or customers that are receiving it do not need to be sold again and again on your products and services, just reminded that you're still there for them in the future!

E-Newsletters:

Technical advancements and web communication have enabled the popularity of the E-newsletter. Can you image if you had the ability to contact all of your clients with one of your most powerful weapons, your newsletters, on demand? Printed newsletters are great, but they take time, energy, and money to produce. Even after you write the stories, collect the photographs, design the layout, and send it to the printer, you still need to get them back for mailing, a process could take weeks or months. With E-newsletters, you're able to do that virtually overnight, or even within a few hours. The only problem that I see with an E-newsletter is that everyone is so inundated today with emails that it might not carry as much weight as a newsletter that you would physically send out. I think this is why I've hesitated to do so in the past. I didn't want to just send out a standard email but wanted to send out something that had a classier look to it. I've received some very impressive emails from Best Buy, Nordstrom, Macy's, and other types of department stores. I've received monthly E-newsletters from Tony Robbins and they look very well done, very classy and to the point, and I look forward to reading them versus just a normal email.

As technology has gotten better, there are a number of different companies that offer this service. The company I use for all of our printing is Marathon Press in Norfolk, Nebraska. They've partnered with a company that has allowed us to create our own E-newsletters right in house, using templates and with the ability to insert photographs and text, sent to clients in the blink of an eye!

In creating this E-newsletter, Marathon Press creates a graphic banner for the top that has, in the case of the studio, "What's new at Hudson's." At the bottom the footer has all of our contact information, including our website, phone number and address. For the main body of the E-newsletter, there are a number of different templates that can be used to insert images and text. It's amazing how easy it is to change the font size, color, and layout.

The beauty of these E-newsletters is the speed with which you can create them. A good example of this is exemplified through our Portrait Safaris. We book a certain date, like the one we do in the fall called "Portraits in the Leaves" on a Saturday and Sunday. We take appointments, then have clients meet us at a park. Saturdays usually fill up fairly quickly and this year we sent traditional newsletters and cards to our clients. Because of this marketing effort, we had only two openings left on Sunday. I thought I'd just try and see if I could get those booked so I put together a very simple E-newsletter with two images from previous years, indicating we only had two openings left. It literally took ten minutes to put this thing together and we were able to email our clients. Within one hour those two available appointments were booked. That's when I truly became a believer in the concept of E-newsletters.

I think that E-newsletters are great for time sensitive material. For instance, we sell gift certificates during the holidays for people needing last minute gift ideas. In the past, we've let people know about gift certificates through traditional newsletters. We would send them out in September and October, but by the time the holiday season rolls around, the message will have been long forgotten. Most people that purchase the gift certificates are looking for something last minute, so this year we sent out an E-newsletter featuring the certificates. We did this a couple of weeks before Christmas and, once again, we got several takers. It was the perfect idea at the perfect time for clients trying to find something to give a loved one for Christmas. This is where E-newsletters really shine.

I have a lot of photographer friends that are down in Texas, and one of their biggest photographic opportunities for people to have portraits, is during the blooming of the blue bonnets in Spring. Blue bonnets are little purple flowers that grow on the side of roads and fields and are very unpredictable as to when they decide to blossom. Nobody really knows when they are going to arrive so booking appointments and taking photographs on specific dates is really difficult. But in the case of an E-newsletter, once you see these little flowers sprout, an E-newsletter is the best way to let clients know the time to take these photographs is right now.

The same type of example can be seen in Washington. Here in western Washington, there are a lot of different flower festivals where the daffodils and tulips are the focus. But with these flowers, sometimes they're at their peak during the festivals and sometimes they're not. With E-newsletters you can react to time sensitive information quickly!

Let's take a look at a business just starting to use the E-newsletter concept in their marketing and the evolution it took to get there, Armondo's Italian Café.

I have had the pleasure of knowing Armondo (Mondo) Pavone for the last 21 years. I'm one of his biggest fans in the community, not just because of his fantastic Italian cuisine, but also for the marketing evolution he has experienced in the last 2 decades.

In 1982, at the age of 19, Mondo started in the food business by helping a friend run a small cookie shop in downtown Seattle. It was called "Just Cookie" and it capitalized on the "Mrs. Fields" nitch that was wildly successful in the early 1980's. They would sell cookies all day with lines of customers going out the doors. He and his partner opened a few more stores and then sold them off in 1984 for a tidy profit.

Mondo envisioned using the same concept with "Just Cookie" and apply it to "Pizza by the Slice." After madly searching for the perfect small location in Seattle with a lot of foot traffic, he decided to come back to his home town of Renton, Washington, just south of Seattle.

A friend of Mondo's had mentioned to him that a restaurant had just gone out of business on a very busy corner of downtown Renton. This location would prove ideal not just because of the foot traffic but vehicle traffic as well.

Mondo's vision was to open a little Italian eatery that served pizza and salad, run it for six to eight months, create some cash flow, sell it, and then move on. He signed the lease July 1st 1985 and for the next 10 months worked odd jobs for friends to scrape enough money for sheetrock, paint, just to get the place open as soon as possible. In May of 1986, Armondo's opened for business. He had 10 tables and could seat only 28. I remember this vividly as my family was one of his first patrons. My kids were 2 and 4 years old at the time and with no hostess we even had the opportunity to seat ourselves. It was fun watching this young 21 year old restaurateur in back cooking up a storm for his eager new customers.

Back then, Mondo's was more interested in creating the menu than marketing and building his clientele. He tried a few marketing ideas but admitted he had no idea what direction to go. 2 years passed and even though he had many regulars who loved him, it wasn't a large enough client base to sustain the business. By now Mondo owed a lot of people money and figured he had about 6 months left before he would have to close. I remember his frustrations at the time, "People who know us, love us", Mondo explained!

One day a local sign painter was working across the street and came in for lunch. He instantly became a huge fan and came back on a regular basis. He convinced Mondo that he needed a new sign out front and proposed it at no charge until his cash flow situation improved. Mondo gratefully accepted and business started to increase. About the same time he traded with the local printing company for a direct mail piece that offered 2 for 1 fettuccine Alfredo, which at the time was his signature dish. Literally in 30 days his business doubled and then in another 30 days tripled!

That point in Armondo's evolution as a restaurant is still fresh in his mind today. He went from barley making it and being in major league debt, to a profitable business ready to move forward, almost overnight.

As the years went by, Armondo's expanded not once, but twice which also included a wine and tap bar with the 3rd expansion. He went from seating 28 guests to 96 guests. Once again Mondo's focus was to build the expanded restaurant, trying to add new customers with your typical marketing strategies rather than maintaining the relationship with his old ones.

During this 11 year period, many things started changing. First, Armondo's was the not the only game in town anymore, numerous quality restaurants opened and appealed to the Renton area, thus giving his customers more dinning options other than Armondo's. He also had the opportunity to open another restaurant, The Melrose Grill. The Melrose features high quality steaks, chops, and seafood in an old historic Renton building built in 1903. For those of you from the East coast and Midwest regions you might be thinking- "That's not that old." But for the Seattle area that is very old. In fact, the building is one of the oldest in my city of Renton. Anyway, as you can imagine starting a restaurant from the ground up takes a lot of time, energy, and money. Mondo had hired managers to watch over and run his Italian place, many of which, sad to say, were not up to par.

During those years Armondo's business started to decline while The Melrose became Renton's newest shinning star. Fortunately Mondo was able to find the *holes in the dike* as I like to call them, and began patching up the damage that had been done the past few years.

This was an extremely stressful time for my friend and I admire him for having the courage to go back to the basics that originally built his business. Remember in the beginning of this story he was going to be in and out in six to eight months?

In the last 20 years Mondo had started Armondo's, expanded twice, opened a second restaurant The Melrose Grill, and I also forgot to mention, acquire thousands of square feet of commercial real estate in Renton. Not bad for a cookie salesman. Ironically he owned most of the block but did not own the space Armondo's occupied. It was an elusive goal to own that prime corner space that Armondo's had been in since the beginning, but it never materialized. So instead of signing a new lease with his landlord, he decided to once again "Go for it", remodel, and move Armondo's to the other end of the block to a space that he owned.

Today the new Armondo's seats 130 guests, has a beautiful full bar, and state of the art kitchen. It is a gorgeous place to dine and my family and I do it quite often!

With Mondo's newest venture also came new challenges for him in his industry. More overhead, and yes, more competing restaurants nipping at his heels. I began this book project during the time in which Armondo's decided to remodel and move. One day we were talking and I mentioned that I was writing a book about relationship marketing and he became very curious. The conversation changed to me asking him, "Mondo, you have been in business 20 years now - How many customers do you have in your database?" "What database?" Armondo answered. I was astonished, "Dude, you don't have a database?"

Armondo replied again, "I have had some managers collect names and addresses on cards over the years but we have never really done anything with them." It was at that point I was writing the chapter about newsletters and e-newsletters. I wanted to share the successful marketing concepts that had allowed my business to keep in touch so well with my clients over the years.

This is when I introduced Mondo to the newest little miracle I had found, the e-newsletter. For only a $200.00 investment, as I mentioned earlier thanks to Marathon Press, and a concerted effort to collect names and email addresses, Armondo's could be in the business of relationship marketing virtually overnight.

With more seats to fill and the increasing competition, Mondo agreed to try the e-newsletter concept. He produced a response card that his servers presented at the end of the meal. It asked for their name, email address, and any other comments they had about their dinning experience. The card also was used as an entry into a drawing for *Dinners for a Year*. In the first 2 weeks 95% of the customers happily participated in the email round up. Mondo found the key to the high percentage was educating their customers why they wanted the information. "We want you to be a part of us-We want to keep you informed of upcoming events-What's new at Armondo and weekly specials, stuff like that."

Customer response from the beginning has been extremely positive. The first e-newsletter sent featured $10 dollars off your dinner upon your next visit and said simply thanks for joining. Mondo uses this same e-newsletter for the first and initial mailing to his customers and new subscribers. This is an awesome idea that I am going to start using in my own business! Creating a dedicated e-newsletter to introduce the concept and basically welcome my new clients to the Hudson's Premiere Portrait family. I have a feeling that Mondo's perfect customers have some of the same characteristics that my perfect clients do. They enjoy keeping in touch, being rewarded for loyalty, and love relationships. Sound familiar?

So at this point in Mondo's marketing journey, he has collected over 3,000 names and addresses. It is his goal to triple this number by the end of 2007! Like in any business there are peaks and valleys through the months and years, or in the restaurant world - weekly. I have enjoyed watching Mondo embrace this relationship marketing concept and utilize it in creative ways. He has a real grasp of who his perfect diners are. In a way he is trying to create a better diner through constant communication and education.

Another goal for Mondo is to change the once a month diner at Armondo's to a weekly one. If Monday or Tuesdays are slow, drive the guests to those evenings and thus fill in the peaks and valleys! One thing Mondo has learned the hard way is that you "Run the risk of driving your bread and butter diners away with to many specials-you have to find a happy medium. Two-fers diners are extremely inconsistent customers. The last thing you want to do is train your diners to become the two for one types. Once again, finding that happy medium."

Finally, sharing this segment has been the most rewarding part of writing this book. I saved this part of the chapter for last to allow Mondo time to experience the success that is possible with e-newsletters and relationship marketing. As he began to see the results he also began to investigate how his restaurant peers might be using this concept as well. The results of his investigations have changed his marketing direction forever. One of Seattle's top restaurateurs and owner of 10 restaurants has been doing e-newsletters for the last couple of years and now has over 60,000 customers in his database. He now exclusively uses e-newsletters for his marketing. As Mondo says so well, "You plagiarize the concepts and ideas from the ones that are successful."

Both Mondo and Armondo's Café Italiano's marketing evolution began from nothing, from 2 for 1 Fettuccine, to today recognizing that relationship marketing is the future of his business. "I have learned you don't really have to worry about the new customers, they are the gravy now!" Sounds like a total 180 degree turn to me! Mondo knew this the whole time of our relationship; I just shared with him a simple, inexpensive vehicle that he was able to plug in to his marketing program instantly. He has taken the e-newsletter concept beyond all my expectations and I know the continued results he will experience will exceed his expectations as well! Thanks, Mondo, for the great friendship, incredible food, and the extra 20 pounds these last 21 years!

6

WELCOME TO THE CLUB

We've been very successful in our business with relationship marketing, in that we keep in touch with our clients as much as possible. We do it through newsletters, cards we send out, letters, and sometimes even just phone calls. We also keep in touch through client dinners, which will get further attention in the chapter Ponies, Popcorn & Pinots.

Years ago there was a downturn in the economy. It seemed like we weren't getting the repeat clientele coming back to the studio as fast as we would have liked. That's when we started looking at what some other industries and businesses were doing to bring back their customers.

We noticed that the airlines especially seemed to be fighting for their customers' loyalty. They were always trying to give an incentive to fly with them more than just once. This is when the 'frequent flyer' concept was born with Delta Airlines and United Airlines and most of the major carriers giving you incentives to book with them. At that time, our carrier of choice was United Airlines. They went to most of the major cities we went to, and we would go out of our way to book with them, just so that we would get those complimentary upgrades and freebies. It's a lot more fun sitting up in front than it is in the back, and when you experience that once or twice, it's really hard to go behind that curtain again.

We began looking at a lot of different clubs and analyzing them, how could we use this in our own business to attract our clients to come back to us more often? So we started our own frequent portrait club with a charity auction and then a Mariner's game.

I love to donate to charity auctions. I love to donate to them from our studio and also attend and spend money at them. It's a win-win for everyone, especially the charity. We donate certificates toward portraits and have large samples of our work on display for potential bidders to see. It's a great way to showcase my photography to several hundred people in the community all at one time. Better yet, we have the wonderful opportunity to give something back to our community.

One of the best items that Sue and I bid on and won was a luxury suite at a Seattle Mariners baseball game. There was room for fourteen people, so Sue and I started thinking about who we should invite. And we thought this is a great way to kind of give back to our clients. We looked at our top clients that we enjoyed working and socializing with, and asked if they would like to come and spend the evening in a Mariners luxury suite watching some baseball.

As Sue and I greeted our top clients that day, one of the gentleman bent over to tie his shoe, and his keys came out of his pocket. He immediately exclaimed, "Don't worry, I'll get them; I'll get the keys. Don't look, don't look!" And as I bent down to pick up the keys for him, I noticed the key ring had a little plastic picture holder that held a wallet size photograph. As I looked closer I noticed a cute picture of his daughters on the key ring… a picture that I hadn't taken. The image appeared to be a "quickie" type picture taken in a mall or department store.

"I didn't want you to see that," he said with chagrin. Making a quick recovery, I proposed, "Well, let's talk about this." Luckily the game wasn't very good so we sat down and talked. "You know," he explained, "We love what you do, and we love your work, but we don't feel like we want to come in and invest what we normally invest every time we see you. That picture was the girls in their Easter dresses, and we didn't want to bother you with something small like that."

That was a valid point but he continued, "We didn't want to spend the kind of money that we always spend with you, just for these kinds of pictures." That was a real eye-opener for both Sue and me, because over the years we tried to create a studio that went from doing the team pictures, the dance pictures, the passport/immigration photos, to a more (as it's called in our business) "carriage-trade studio," that dealt with clients who really wanted to invest top dollar in their portraits. We started thinking that maybe we took that concept too far, because we didn't do Easter pictures, we didn't do Santa pictures because we were, well, not to sound stuffy, but *maybe* we were the type of studio that just wouldn't do those kinds of things anymore. So this was a significant realization to what the possibilities were with our studio.

During the course of the game, Sue and I sat down with this couple and the other couples there, which was great. It was almost like we had a focus group where we could ask questions of our clients. What we gained that day was the understanding that you have a number of clients that are really good clients. They like to come back, and they like to spend money with you; and what kind of thank you could we give them, similar to a frequent flier program. That night we came up with a concept that we call the *Premier Portrait Club*, and the concept is: the more they use us, the more perks and pricing incentives we give them.

Some of the advantages we decided for our Premiers were not charging them to be a part of this club, like a positive 'thank you for all your years of loyalty to us.' Another perk was that they would not have to pay a session fee anymore.[1] This has been pretty major for our clients. We have found over the years that people will come in a lot more frequently if they know they don't have to pay that up-front session fee, even though it is a small percentage of the total cost that they're going to be paying for that particular portrait.

THE RELATIONOGRAPHER

Another big incentive that we decided to offer our club members is in the portrait pricing department. With our normal prices, we have a two-tiered pricing with our smaller prints, like 8x10's and 5x7's. Once a client invests in what we call a wall portrait, which in our studio is a 16x20 or larger, the smaller prints like 8x10's and 5x7's will come down in price to half. We decided to let our Premiers, whether or not they do invest in that larger portrait, have that second-tier pricing. So then, along with not paying a session fee they also don't have to invest in a larger portrait, they can just get the smaller ones. What we found out is that also added to the frequency of them coming back to our studio. And what's really ironic is that, in most cases, they usually invest in a larger portrait, because they have other large portraits in their home, and over the years they have enjoyed those portraits; they truly believe in photography as an art form, and it's kind of hard to have an 8x10 or 5x7 on the wall and really consider that art. And because they're Premier Portrait Club members, along with that second-tier pricing incentive, we also give them an automatic 10% off on large wall portraiture and 15% off frames.

Another feature we developed for the Premier Portrait Club was hosting Santa portraits and Easter portraits, and in some cases we would do Halloween portraits too. Normally, everything that we sell at the studio is ala carte, meaning they're going to buy each image separately. Consequently that package is going to be only a fraction of what they normally pay at the studio. But in the case of, for example, going to Santa pictures at the mall, our quality is going to be far superior to mall photos. It's a trade-off for them. Maybe they're paying $25 at the mall, and with us they're paying $125, but the experience we give them is far superior to what they're going to get at the mall, where they may have to wait up to two hours with increasingly cranky kids. With us, they're going to schedule an appointment just for themselves, and we've got the Christmas music playing, we have cookies and cider for the kids, and champagne for the parents, it's just a wonderful experience. If little Johnny's afraid of Santa, he can go out in the lobby and have another cookie and give it another go in twenty minutes or so. It's a wonderful experience all around.

As far as our bottom line goes, we didn't really see these special events with Santa and Easter as being a real money-maker; it wasn't something that we *had* to make money at, it was more giving back to our clients and giving *them* a good experience, and pretty much just saying, 'thank you so much for being our client all these years.'

Over the years, we've put together a package of incentives or 'perks' for our Premier Portrait Club members which has worked extremely well. With the marketing through E-newsletters, we are able to keep in touch with our clients even better. Along with our three hundred or so Premier Portrait Club members, we are now also in the process of collecting Email addresses from *all* of the clients in our database, because we are so pleased with the success of our E-newsletter, which is so perfect for time sensitive events.

Who's in it?

So by now you're probably wondering, *who gets to be in this club?* By the time we started our Premier Portrait Club, we had become pretty good at collecting names and addresses for our database. We started looking at the list of our clients and deciding, first of all, *who had invested good sums of money with us?* Another criterion was, *who did we like to work with?*

Today I have to say, almost every client I work with, I love to work with. But back in the earlier days, we had a few stinkers whom we would rather not work with and those are usually the ones that we don't send anything to. In fact, I can remember when Sue particularly frustrated with one client who upset her, and she asked, "Why do we even keep in touch with this person? We don't want to work with them." That night, we sat down and went through our client list, and we deleted all the people that we didn't want to come back to the studio.

As our studio has progressed and our prices have increased, the quality of our clients has also improved. I don't mean that in a social way; I mean their attitude and excitement to work with us while happily investing in my work. That, by the way, has changed as well. When we first started we were the cheapest studio in the area with flawed experience and they came to us because of price, not necessarily because of the artistic quality and service.

One of the criteria for becoming a club member is that we'll look at what they've spent in the past. Another thing we consider is that relationship; in most cases, a lot of my clients start out as high school seniors. They're 17 or 18 years old, and if I do a good job on their senior portrait session, they will remember us and return for their wedding and family portraits. Currently 80% of the weddings I do are former high school senior clients, and I attribute that to relationship marketing, beginning with that wonderful experience the first time they came in my door.

Right now in my career, and I've been doing this 25 years, I am now photographing a lot of high school seniors whose *parents wedding* I photographed 18-25 years ago! That's very cool. That's the good news. The bad news is in some cases I have not even *seen* these clients in 18 or 25 years. I can attribute that to the fact that when we first started out, we were not good at relationship marketing. We did not keep in touch, and thus lost track of them. It's only been in the last fifteen years or so that we've actually done a good job with this relationship marketing. So to me, it shows how important it is to keep in touch with your clients.

So past relationships is another criterion for who we select to be in the club. They're people that we've worked with over and over again, they have a great attitude, they love working with us, and they're also the people who give us a lot of referrals.

However, in some cases, it might take only one session with a client, in which they really enjoyed what we did, and we really enjoyed working with them. At that moment we might instantly tell them, "Welcome to the club!" and then explain some of the wonderful incentives for becoming such a great client.

WELCOME TO THE CLUB

Other great examples of clubs

I enjoy wine and I really enjoy touring wineries in Napa, California. It's amazing to observe the enormous competition that wineries deal with. Napa is an absolutely gorgeous place, and if you go there during the harvest and "crush" in early October, the smell of the valley is just majestic. The competition forces each winery to be unique, to try to do something to give some notoriety to themselves, and to make them stand out from the others. You get certain wineries, like *Cakebread Cellars*, who will not trim their Sauvignon Blanc vines back. That prevents the Sauvignon Blanc grapes from getting sunburned, and that's supposed to help the flavor of that particular wine. If you head north up the road to another favorite winery of mine, which is *Frog's Leap*, they don't use any chemicals, fertilizers, or pesticides. In fact, they don't even water. Instead, they use the old-fashioned method of farming, where the vines grow 20 feet deep to get the water, so that wine doesn't have soil that they say is *poisoned*, and that helps with the flavor of the wine.

Each winery has their niche, and each try to stand out from their competition. That kind of competition, where everybody is so close to each other, and doing virtually the same thing and selling the same product, has been the catalyst to spawn a great system of wine clubs. You join this club, which in most cases you don't have to pay for, and you have a list of incentives for buying their wines. In some cases, they're going send you a shipment of their new releases; maybe it's once a month, maybe it's once every two months or six months, depending on how they have it set up, but boy, talk about loyalty.

One of the clubs I belong to is *Cakebread Cellars*. It's a wonderful winery, with the feeling of a boutique winery. These wineries are somewhat smaller operations, more family-owned, and tend to harvest most of the grapes in their own vineyards and don't buy a lot of grapes from other growers. It's all done mainly in-house, so to speak. Still they have a fairly large production, even with this feeling of a boutique winery.

THE RELATIONOGRAPHER

When you visit most wineries, they have hours of operation for visiting and tastings. At some of the more "boutique" wineries, you have to make appointments to have tours and wine tasting. At *Cakebread Cellars*, even though they produce quite a bit of wine, they still like to have people call ahead for tours and tasting. If you're a club member, you can just walk in and show them your card, and they treat you like you're one of the major stockholders, which is a great feeling. As a member they waive the appointment rule, there is no charge for the wine tasting (which include a better selection of wine), and members get an additional percentage off any wine. It makes me want to come back there!

Nearly all wineries now charge for tasting, and in most cases have different levels of tasting. There are the entry-level wines, where you might get four or five different types of wines; they're showing what their new release is, and the tasting might be 15 dollars for that. That's pretty common. But if you are a member of their club, there is no fee. That's at the entry level. Occasionally they will bring out the more expensive wines, what they call library wines, and usually those tastings are even more expensive. Once again, because you're a member, there is no cost, but a reward for your loyalty.

Those are some of the really neat added perks. Of course, anything that you purchase at that winery while you're there will be discounted because you're a member. In fact, we joined one club down there, where a members purchase might normally get 25% off their regular prices, but with a new members first purchase, they gave us 40% off. Certainly that gave us an incentive to buy a couple of cases, when you're getting that kind of first-purchase discount.

It's amazing how successful these wine clubs are, proven by the fact that some of the smaller wineries don't even distribute their product. You don't see them in restaurants, you don't see them in stores, but they actually sell out of particular wines *just* to their club members. That's an amazing to feat to think that here they don't have to do any additional work for distributing or marketing certain types of products because they're already pre-sold basically as soon as they're produced. That's a wonderful position to be in.

When you walk into a winery, you see a general tasting area for non-club members, or people that are just there on a tour. As a club member, they offer a special area if you prefer, and it can be just for one or two people. They'll take you over to seperate area with a special table, with your own waiter who's very knowledgeable about the wines. And rather then a "belly up to the bar" situation, where you're with a bunch of people you don't know, and the person pouring is trying to talk to everyone, you have a much more intimate experience as a member of that club.

Cakebread Cellars, along with some other wine clubs that I belong to, ship your wine with their newsletter. They also have a detailed description of what that wine is. When I say detailed, it's things like, when the grapes were harvested, at what PH level and sugar level, and the wine maker did this to it and did that to it, etc. For people who are really into wine, it's fascinating to learn the characteristics of the wine, and why it is what it is. The newsletter provides interesting information about things such as when they planted, or if they're harvesting, or they're pruning, or invitations to special events that club members may attend. A lot of the shipments also include recipes, and if you've never been to Napa, you know that some of the best restaurants in the country are located there. In fact, there's a whole movement of good wine and good food in that valley. Those recipes seem like such a simple little thing, but in my mind, they increase the value of what they're sending you as a benefit of club membership.

Cakebread Cellars wine club has really taken the club concept to the next level, and in my opinion, is probably one of the best wine clubs in Napa valley, not that I'm a member of all of them but I'm a member of quite a few. Recently I had the opportunity to go to one of their events at the winery, the open house to release their new wines. After speaking with the owners I was amazed to hear they had close to 9,000 members in the club. The event was on a Saturday and Sunday, and from what I observed had just 900 tickets available on Saturday and 900 tickets available on Sunday, primarily for the wine club members. As members passed through the entrance, we were given name tags and were checked off the list. Grabbed a glass, and then the fun began! We were actually in the large barrel rooms of the winery and there were a lot of people there, and a lot of wine. You had to be patient, but it was fun talking to people you'd never met before while in line. They'd talk about their love for wine and food and also for *Cakebread Cellars*. As we were traveling through the line they had different wine stations. One of the wonderful aspects of this event was the executive chef preparing the perfect food pairings and entrees for each wine. You received a program for the event with all of the recipes and details of the wine you were tasting. As we strolled through the Sauvignon Blanc's, Chardonnays, Merlots, and Cabernets it made for a delightful experience as a club member. I can't wait till next year's open house!

I think the one thing that *Cakebread Cellars* has figured out, that we also figured out in our own business, is that the people part of this club, in our case it is our *Premier Portrait Club*, have much of the same life characteristics as other club members. They like good wine, good food, and a good time. It is like my perfect clients that belong to our *Premier Portrait Club*, they are all out of a similar mold. What *Cakebread Cellars* has done is take the club concept to a whole new level for their club members. They provide opportunities to go to different areas of the country. For example, travel to Alaska to go salmon fishing on a Friday or Saturday and then on Sunday, learn how to prepare your catch, and pair it with the perfect wine. This becomes an event for the club members to experience together. They also have an event in Houston, Texas where they are able to enjoy Texan cuisine and then later on, all go together to a rodeo. There is an opportunity to also go to Spring Training and a round of golf in Phoenix, Arizona. From coast to coast *Cakebread Cellars* intrigues its members with its variety of events. It's the ultimate club experience with people who have the same tastes as you. It was amazing to watch while we were in line at the open house people who actually knew each other because they had been to these events together many times. A lot of lifelong friendships have come out of it.

Another example of having clubs going away together, if you want to call it that, is with the company I mentioned before, *Marathon Press*. About half of their business is with photographers, creating brochures, cards, and any printing needs. They also have begun producing websites and E-newsletters. They have a program called the *MVP Program* which is a two year commitment. You an established fee each month for various marketing materials to be used in your business, at a reduced cost. *MVP* is a group of photographers that are very committed to marketing, are very serious about marketing, and understand that marketing is something you have to do on a daily basis, not just something you do when business is slow. They offer MVP customers a marketing getaway every year. Some of these getaways have been in such places as Santa Fe, Breckenridge, San Diego, and this year they are going to be down in Napa Valley. These are a little bit of education, with a lot of good fellowship and experiences together. It brings photographers together from all over the country to share ideas. They have speakers and break out sessions to discuss what's working in their part of the country, how to increase their market share and gain new clients and specifically how to maintain the ones they have using relationship marketing. I think it's a great way to promote their agenda and to maintain that relationship with their very best customers, which are part of that MVP program.

The frequent user concept is even used with vacation travel. Several years ago, I had the opportunity to go on a ten-day cruise. This particular cruise line was Holland America. At Holland America they have a different kind of clientele and a different kind of demographic they go after. In the most part, the cruisers that go on Holland America are very experienced cruisers. I would say the average age was probably 55 to 75 years of age, up every morning walking around the deck, very fit. Most are retired folks but these are people who have time to spend on the ship. The thing that was a little different about Holland America, as I found out, was that many of the passengers that had been on the ship for a long time. In fact, I recall that rumors claimed there was one couple who had been on numerous Alaska cruises, then traveled from Alaska to the Caribbean, and while in transit down to the Caribbean, had been on various Caribbean Cruises. In other words, they had an almost semi-permanent residence on board. I had never heard about that before. During the week, though, I found out how it was done. You pay $2,500.00 for a ten-day cruise, and then during that week, they offer you the chance to stay on the ship for another week for half of that. Of course if you have the money and you have the time, this is a great way to travel and to live. As I see it, this is primarily the type of customer Holland America is catering to.

For those passengers, the club concept becomes exceedingly valuable. I think it's not just for the perks, though I'm sure they get quite a few, but also for the prestige. The thing that was really interesting was that they had a couple of special events on the ship where these frequent cruise passengers would attend special cocktail parties and dinner parties with the captain, and it was a very special thing to them. It was more of a status thing, than just about saving money. In fact, they award these big medallions for passengers who have had a hundred nights, or two hundred nights, or three hundred nights on a Holland America Cruise.

Another thing I noticed about these clubs, especially the cruise ship club, was that it seemed like a lot of these people knew each other; perhaps from past other cruises, they became friends on board. Typically, they appear to be in the same type of social/economic situation; a lot of them have the same type of philosophies; and just as an observation, it seems like people in general tend to join clubs that have people who think like them and do the same things they do. I know that in a lot of trade associations, such as The Professional Photographers of America, photographers love to get together and talk about what they're doing and how they're doing it, and I think that *might* be one of the things with these clubs—that it's not just the money incentives and extra perks, but just being considered a part of a group, a part of a culture, if you will.

These frequent flyer, frequent drinker, or frequent photo clubs are great ways to say thank you to not only your best clients, but to all your clients. I think the mileage clubs have done a great job of heightening the perks as the air miles grow. The more times you fly with them the more opportunities you have to fly first class or fly free. With our particular portrait club we handle it a little differently in that we reserve it for our very best clients. These clients have shown such loyalty and patronage over the years we want to reward them.

The remarkable thing about clubs such as United, Holland America, and Cakebread Cellars is that they are a *turn key system*. Those perks are designed to be automatic in which the system is in place, you don't have to think about giving customers/clients their rewards for things they may be purchasing or investing in. With the mileage clubs of the airlines, the more flights you take with them the more opportunities you have to get free flights or those free upgrades. In contrast, with our portrait club we save the reward our exclusive clients that have benefited from the beginning.

You can treat all clients equally. You don't give favoritism over one customer or the other, which was something I had problems with when we first started our business. Clients who came back on a consistent or regular basis, we developed particular relationships with. We felt that we wanted to reward and thank them differently so we would give them a certain percentage off, or a free frame. The Premier Portrait Club and the way we have structured it we treat everyone equally.

I've noticed that the people in these clubs are the type of people who appreciate being rewarded for their loyalty. They become walking, talking billboards for that company, may it be with United or Cakebread cellars, or with Holland America. They are the kind of people who like to shop with a certain vendor, or use a certain service and they are very much appreciated when that company rewards them in a positive way.

This gets back to one of the characteristics of our perfect client profile: they do appreciate the rewards of being loyal.

Lastly, one of the things I've observed with this type of concept, like our own Premier Portrait Club or with these other clubs, is that the group of people that are members of these clubs like to be surrounded with people that have the same kind of passions and interests that they do. A good example of this is watching when we have Santa pictures, watching the premier clients in the lobby networking and socializing. It's just amazing the molds of those people's characteristics are so similar that they get along extremely well. A lot of life-long friendships have formed in the lobby at my studio over the years because the same people see each other. That's something that is truly amazing. I also saw such socializing while standing in line at Cakebread Cellars' open house. People tha didn't know each other, socializing because they share the same interests, in this case for great wine and great food. People like to belong; they like to be around people that they feel are like themselves. I think that not only is this a great way to reward your clients by giving back to them in a structured way, it's also a way for them to socialize and be around people they enjoy.

---

[1] A session fee is a front-end charge that clients pay to have the portrait created. And compared to what they spend on the actual photographs, a session fee is usually a pretty small percentage.

7

IT'S THE 'LITTLE THINGS'

As I mentioned in an earlier chapter, "Starting the Relationship—Creating the Experience", it doesn't take a mega budget to make a memorable experience. Many a client or customer relationship has started from something that was considered small. It could be just a phone call, a fresh apple in a bowl as you check into your hotel, or a thank you card. Sometimes it's the little things that can prove to have the most impact with just impressions or more importantly, maintaining a relationship. This chapter explores lots of little things that various companies and businesses are currently using with much success to enhance the client/customer experience.

Thank You

The first idea is something we have all been taught at a young age and is probably the easiest to perform: just saying thank you! I am a firm believer that just a simple "Thank You" is a very powerful way of keeping in touch with your clients. I know at our studio, it's something that we have done from the very beginning, something I know we strive to do better and better all the time. I can't say that we do it perfect all the time, because it takes a lot of discipline, but we try to send out thank you cards after we've met with the client, after they've placed an order, and then again when they pick their order up.

A personalized thank you has a lot of value for the amount of time and money that you put into it. I can not tell you how many times I've been at a grocery store or the shopping mall and a mom of a high school senior, whose portraits I did, comes up and says, "I just want to thank you for the little note you sent Johnny, it really made his day."

When I am photographing a client, it is my goal to build rapport as quick as I possibly can. I want to get to know them and it is always fun asking them what their plans are for the future, where they work, and what they are doing over the summer. Most of the sessions last about an hour, and during the time I am photographing them, I try to learn as much as I can not just because I want them to be my clients in the future but also, as mentioned earlier in the book, the more questions you ask, the more people feel that you care about them. And it seems at least with photography, the more questions you ask and the more rapport I am able to develop, the more at ease the client feels. I use this same concept of rapport building with my wedding and family clients as well. I usually meet with my wedding and family portrait clients prior to their session, unlike seniors. This enables us to connect, brainstorm, plan their photography experience, and begin the relationship process!

Photographing high school seniors is a little different because I don't require a pre-consultation. This is due to the higher volume of sessions per day and more high school seniors already understand the game plan. This is partly because we have done a great job over the years of educating our clients by sending brochures that include information on how to prepare for their senior session. In most cases, the first time I actually meet my senior client is during the session. Basically the point I am trying to get at here is, the more comfortable your client becomes, the more they relax. When they are relaxed it is more likely for them to give you a natural expression and thus a higher quality photograph.

After the session ends, I am able to take those answers given to me from some of the "get to know you" questions that I asked during the session. I then transfer those over to them in the form of a thank you card: Thank you for coming, thank you for choosing us to photograph your senior year and good luck at Washington State University. By simply adding that personal touch, rather than just sending a generic card that says, "Thank you for your business" and signed at the bottom, is something that definitely carries more weight in the eyes of the customer. I know it seems like a very small thing, but it really is the little things that matter.

So what are some other forms of thank you's? Well, back in the 1980's we did a lot of boudoir photography, which is lingerie and intimate portraits of women for their boyfriend or husband. It was a fun opportunity because instead of just sending a thank you, often we felt it more appropriate to send flowers. Due to the intimate nature of the photography we were creating, flowers were more of a proper way to say thank you. After the session we would find out where they worked and have the flowers sent directly there, so as not to spoil the surprise the photographs usually were for. From all the comments and reactions of our boudoir clients, the flowers were a huge hit. Can you imagine a delivery person bringing these beautiful flowers into an office area and having all the eyes in the room watching to see who receives them? During the next coffee break, the client would be swarmed by her co-workers, "Did they come from your husband?" "No they came from my photographer!" And of course everyone asks, "Well, who is that?"

We found that this form of thank you was always very effective in not only making the client feel special, but also marketing our business as one that is unique in the industry.

If we unfortunately learn there has been a death in the family of one of my client's, we do our best to send something out to let them know that we are thinking of them. I guess that is not really a thank you per se, but I think it's a way of doing the right thing, and it works very well. Is it relationship marketing? You bet it is! The whole idea is letting your clients know that they are part of a larger family; they're part of *our* family and we are thinking of them.

Another good example of a thank you (or just checking on you) is from my dentist, Dr. Danny Rude. I have been going to him since the late 1970's. It has been a blast working with him over the years and he has become a great client of mine as well. I truly enjoy photographing his family. In fact, his son Joel, whom I have known since he was young, is now poking around my mouth himself. Now a dentist himself, it's a little scary, remembering him as a little kid and now as one of my dentists!

I'll never forget the time that I had my very first crown made. As they do when they create a crown, they put a temporary one in to start with. Later that week I was at a restaurant and apparently ate something that did not agree with my temporary crown and it fell out. I called Dr. Danny with this exposed root in my mouth (I am kind of a dental wimp when it comes to this stuff anyway) and even though it was the weekend, Dr. Danny stopped what he was doing and said, "Meet me at my office." Because it was a Sunday, he was not able to get a hold of his assistant to help replace my crown. He was amazing as he single handedly got the job done. Of course my favorite gas did make the process go smoothly as well! After my root and crown were fixed I received a call that night at my home. It was Dr. Danny asking how I was feeling and making sure the experience was not too traumatic for me. What a nice touch that he actually took the time, not only on a Sunday to help me, but to also call later that night just to make sure I was feeling ok. That is a class act.

My chiropractor Dr. Scott Petett also gives "thank you's" in a genuine way as well. Scott is a very good marketer, always looking for new patients and he is a marvelous chiropractor to boot. I referred one of my friends to him and a couple of days later that friend went in for his first exam. He instantly became a patient of Scott's and I received a card from him thanking me for referring a new client. Not only was the gesture of the thank you card nice, Scott gave me a $25 gift certificate for a local restaurant I love. Way to go Scott! I would have obviously sent my friend to him without that certificate, but it was just an extra added thank you for referring that patient to him.

I recently received a wonderful gift from a good friend and client of mine, Keith Lee. You will be getting to know Keith in the upcoming chapter Relationship Masters. The gift was a small but powerful book called, <u>The Simple Truths of Service: Inspired by Johnny the Bagger</u>, by Ken Blanchard and Barbara Glanz. It is an inspirational true story about a young man with Downs syndrome who changed the culture and attitude of a grocery store.

Johnny's job is to bag the groceries. He adds his personal touch for each customer by sharing an inspirational quote that he finds on the internet and prints every night before work and inserts into every customer's bag. Store patrons choose to wait in long lines just to receive his daily message! Many of his fans shop multiple times during the week instead of their usual schedule. Johnny's one simple idea transformed an entire business and created an on going relationship that is contagious! Every employee of the store began doing the little extras and going the extra mile for their shoppers, all because Johnny, a simple bagger, took the risk to do something special. What ideas can you come up with to change your business overnight like Johnny did?

I have put together a collection of little things that we use and some genius ideas that I have observed in the general market place. Remember, sometimes it is the little things that are the most effective and have the largest impact.

Hy-Vee Grocery Stores

On a recent trip to Norfolk, Nebraska with my son Josh, we stopped in at a grocery store called Hy-Vee. We do not have Hy-Vee's in the Seattle are so it was a new experience for us. They had a separate liquor, wine, and beer store adjacent to the grocery area. The minute we walked in we both looked at each other and said, "This isn't your typical grocery store." One of the things I was impressed with was the huge variety of wine they offered. They had a giant barrel wine chiller that you could use while checking out that chilled the wine almost instantly. The only other place I have seen this chiller before was in a little boutique wine shop located in Cannon Beach, Oregon. It was very impressive to see this in Nebraska. The beer selection featured domestic, microbrews, and hard to find foreign beers that neither of us have seen since the last time we were in Europe or in a specialty pub in Seattle. The coolest thing was you could mix and match beer in your very own custom six pack and try a little bit of everything. Very cool!

On this same trip to Nebraska, Josh got to check out a Sonic Drive-In for the first time.

Sonic- Specialty Drinks

Sonic Drive Inn, what makes them so special – this is just a hamburger joint right? What Burger King was able to do with the burger "Have it your way" in the 1970's, Sonic has done with the drink. Their tagline is "Your ultimate drink stop" where you can "Customize and flavorize". The back of the Sonic drink cup reads: "At Sonic, we believe in your individual choice, and in the spirit of choice, we offer you 168,894 possible drink combinations, think about it. Starting with an orange vanilla sprite, you could have a different drink everyday for the next 462 years. How's that for refreshing choices!" You can mix and match flavors to anything you want such as: Lemon, Lime, Vanilla, Chocolate, Apple juice, Cherry, Grape, Watermelon, Blue Coconut, Orange, Cranberry, Strawberry, Low Calorie Diet Cherry, Pineapple, Poweraide, and Bubble Gum. My personal favorite is diet cherry lime-aide! That is a great example of 168,894 little things.

Salty's Binoculars

There is a favorite restaurant of mine in Seattle that is known for its seafood. The place is called Salty's. The view of the Seattle skyline is very unique because you look across Elliot Bay on the Puget Sound, a view of Seattle not everyone gets to experience. It is a popular destination for not only tourists but local Seattleites because of the amazing view and fresh seafood. I do a lot of evening portrait sessions in that area because of the spectacular backdrop. Like I said, the place is not only popular with tourists but the locals and my clients as well, so I have spent many nights there.

The last time I had dinner at Salty's after a session I noticed a waiter talking with one of the guests, pointing out landmarks of the city from across the water. Not a moment later the waiter returned with a small pair of binoculars that had the Salty's logo on it! What a great idea! As I became more observant around my table, I noticed that many of the guests were enjoying the same little benefit of dinning at Salty's! It is this little thing that not only enhances ones view of Seattle but their dinning and Seattle experience as a whole.

Travel Hosts - Newark Airport and the Red Jackets

I recently headed back East for a meeting with Fuji Film USA in New York. My destination airport was Newark, not my favorite airport to say the least. They've done some updating but the airport still is very spread out and difficult to navigate. I arrived after 10:00pm not looking forward to the hassle of getting to my bags, picking up a rent-a-car, and driving to my hotel because the Newark airport is so spread out with trams. It makes it difficult to get anywhere. While I was waiting for my bags, I noticed a number of banners promoting their travel hosts dressed in bright red jackets wearing "Ask me for help" buttons. "That was kind of cool" I said to myself. Just then one of the red jackets appeared and asked, "Can I help you with any directions tonight?" Way cool! The travel host pointed me in the direction of the tram I needed to take to go to the rental car area. "Have a nice stay in the area", he exclaimed! Wait a minute; was this really the Newark airport? As I reached the top of the escalator and the boarding area for my tram, there was another helpful red jacket travel host just waiting to assist me. By now it was about 11:00pm. She directed me to the proper train and wished me well. The 5 minute or so ride took me to the end of the line where I was to pick up my rental car. The minute the door to the tram opened, a smiling red jacket in a cheery voice said, "You made it. Congratulations!"

I am sure that Newark is not the only airport in the country that has this service, but for a weary traveler like myself, the red jackets preformed exceptionally. Just a little thing, like giving directions, that went a very long way. I am now looking forward to my next trip to Newark airport.

Barrier Motors - Free Carwashes for Life

I recently purchased a new car at Barrier Motors in Bellevue, Washington. It is an amazing dealership. In fact I'll be showcasing them in an up coming chapter, "Relationship Masters". One of the unique benefits when buying a car from Barrier is the free carwashes for life. Barrier Motors exclusively sells luxury vehicles like Volvo, Mercedes, BMW, Porsche, and Audi. They invested in a state of the art washing facility for the dealership vehicles. But they also designated a couple of stalls for their customers as well. As long as you have a Barrier license plate cover or sticker in the inside door of your car, you can keep it clean for life.

From the relationship marketing stand point this is huge. Each time you travel to wash your car (with their brushless system that will not scratch your beautiful new or pre-owned car like many of the other car washing facilities), you have to drive by all of the Barrier Motors dealerships. May it be a month or a year after your purchase, you will be curious to stop in so conveniently (just for a moment) to see the latest, greatest model.

Stephanie Lorenz

Another person you will be meeting in an up coming chapter Ponies, Popcorn, and Pinots is Real Estate Agent Stephanie Lorenz. You will hear more how I met Steph and how I have worked with her. I have two ideas that I am going to share with you that she does well to maintain the relationship with her clients.

IT'S THE 'LITTLE THINGS'

The first is a letter Stephanie sends out to her clients reminds them of the original purchase price of their home, and better yet, what it is worth in today's market. In the Seattle area real estate market this could result in a 15-25% increase per year! This is great peace of mind for Stephanie's clients and also shows instantly the current equity position of the home owner. This in turn may lead to a future upgrade of home or pulling equity out for investment property.

Stephanie has also put together a scrapbook of cards, letters, and thank you's that her clients have sent to her. We all know that testimonials are sometimes the best form of marketing. It definitely falls in the category of building and nurturing relationships with clients. The scrapbook serves as a great selling piece in her office for new clients to view and is popular with her current and past clients when visiting.

More Realtor Stuff...

The competition with realtors is fierce, especially in the Seattle area as I mentioned before. Home values have been increasing rapidly over the past several years. Everybody's brother, mother, and pastor are all now agents. I know this first hand because I live with one, Terri Arnold. Terri started her career a couple of years ago at the height of the real estate boom. She has been working hard building her business in spite of all the competition. I have learned a term from realtors that they use called "Farming." They select a specific area, like a neighborhood, to market to. The realty world has been on the cutting edge of keeping in touch with their clients as well as past clients. There are hundreds of companies that cater to the real estate profession, supplying them with all kinds of specific items. Pens, water bottles, envelope openers, and much more. I think it is a wonderful way to say thanks and keep in touch but many of the items have little to no value. Terri has found a unique item that is both very cost effective and has lasting value.

She sends out football and baseball schedules that have a magnet stripe on the back. It also has a place for a standard business card that can be attached with nothing more than double sided tape. The finished product looks great printed in 4 color. In the spring Terri sends out the Seattle Mariners schedule and in the late summer she sends out the Washington State Cougars, University of Washington Huskies, and the one that everyone can agree upon, the Seattle Seahawks schedules. This little thing cost about $1.25 including postage, but has incredible value and shelf life. Good job Terri!

Apple Capital

Have you ever visited the State of Washington? Of course I am biased, but I would never want to live anywhere else. If you do someday travel to Washington, try and make your way to the center of the state, to the City of Wenatchee. Wenatchee is the apple capital of the world. I am in Wenatchee (3 hours from Seattle) 2-3 times a year working with one of my favorite clients. I usually stay at the Westcoast Hotel right downtown. Available to you when you check in is a big bowl of fresh, juicy Washington State apples. Yes, its just apples but I think it is a special way to say welcome to Wenatchee and apple country.

Lots & Lots of Goodies

I think the key to making the "Little things" concept work is finding a value item that is cost effective. This is what I have tried to do over the years in my business. Here are a few examples from what I have done for the "Little things."

For high school seniors we have given t-shirts with their class year on them, license plate covers (again with their graduating year on them), and my recent favorite, a tri-color highlighter with "Hudson Designer Portraits - The Highlight of your Senior Year!" printed on them. (Terri gets the credit here. It was her idea!)

For our family portraits, and weddings clients we have our Hudson's Designer Roast Coffee. I know you're thinking Seattle is the coffee capital, and you're right! We give away a half pound bag of fresh roasted coffee beans with our own custom label. A client of mine Brett Habineck owns Java Java Coffee Co.—you'll meet him later in the chapters "Ponies, Popcorn and Pinots" and "Relationship Masters"—and he provides us with this wonderful coffee.

Remember value right? Well I decided to spend the $0.25 more and upgrade to the sport water bottle. These water bottles are reusable, which has a longer shelf life, equals more value to the client.

Terri and I recently returned from Italy. As we were flying back, we tried to come up with a way to share the images that we created with our family, friends, and both of our clients. We came up with a calendar idea. Not just a homemade Kinko's or Sam's Club style calendar, but a professionally designed and printed gem that could compete with any cute puppy or Sports Illustrated Swimsuit calendar! We used the talented graphic designer Stephanie Dejong, a client and friend of Terri and I. She did the layout at MarathonPress.com, and then was printed by them at their base in Norfolk, Nebraska. It turned out so well that it will be in the marketing budget for coming years.

Once we have finished with a client and everything's been delivered we choose an image from their session and create custom note cards. It is basically custom stationary with the client's very own image printed on it. Using Photoshop the image is filtered to look like a water color painting. Not only is it a great thank you but it is also a way for our clients friends and family to see our work in a more fine art kind of way.

Become a Magician

I have a photographer friend in Tacoma, WA that has been in the business about as long as I have. Recently I discovered that he is an accomplished professional magician. Not just a hobby but doing shows on a professional level. The best part of the story is that he has incorporated his magical talents into his photography business as well. The biggest challenge of being a portrait photographer is making people relax in front of the camera, especially children. What better way to enhance the experience of a portrait session then by being entertained by a magician!

Local Legend- Les Schwab

We have a legendary tire store in the Pacific Northwest called Les Schwab Tires. Why are they legendary? Because of their passion for the customer! I first experienced the Les Schwab experience when I was in college up in Bellingham, WA. Sue and I had a flat tire to deal with and one of my friends mentioned Les Schwab tires. "Go to Les Schwab, they will change the tire for free", he said. "No way- even if the tire didn't come from Les Schwab", I asked? He was right, so we took our 1965 Ford Mustang to Les Schwab and they fixed it! That was our first experience, but not our last. Anytime I even think of putting tires on my car, I go to Les Schwab.

Here are some more "Little things" that Les Schwab adds to the experience. First of all, when ever you pull up to a Les Schwab Tires store, you are always greeted at your door by one of their technicians. Not only do they greet you but they run out to your car. On top of that, when it is raining, as it does frequently in our part of the country, you are greeted with an umbrella. You always see the technicians hustling all over the store, ready to serve you.

Another "Little thing" is a long tradition called "Free Beef" that takes place in February at all their stores. I know it sounds crazy, but when you buy new tires in the month of February, you get to go to the freezer in the lobby and pull out a couple of steaks for each tire purchase. How do I know this? I participated last February and the steaks were good too! And as an added choice, you can choose to receive a sampler pack with salami, jerky, and beef sticks instead of the steaks. This is just another added bonus for non-steak lovers.

All of the "Little things" that Les Schwab Tire does for its customers has paid off. They started in the small town of Princeville, Oregon in 1952. Today they're one of the largest independent tire dealers in the United States with more than 7,000 employees and 400 stores throughout Oregon, Washington, Idaho, Montana, Nevada, Alaska, and Utah! For me it started with a flat and continues with free beef 30 years later. Check them out at lesschwab.com. There is even a book about Les Schwab and how he started his amazing company.

There are "Little things" all around us that can increase the perceived value of our product or service. These little things can also transform an average experience into a memorable one. Once you're aware of all the tremendous ideas that are out there, you'll realize the marketing opportunities are endless! The key is to recognize the good ideas and mold them into your own business.

I began to realize this when I became a passionate student of marketing. There has not been a day that goes by where I haven't learned or experienced an idea on a plane, in a magazine, or just by being observant in the market place to a concept that I couldn't transfer into my own business. Do I sound possessed? I feel in a way I am. I challenge you to become as possessed in your search for the "Little things" to keep in touch and enhance your own business or service.

8

PONIES, POPCORN AND PINOTS
"Sometimes saying *thank you* is just not enough"

Authors Note: I'm turning a total 180 degrees from the last chapter! Sorry, BH

What better way to say 'thank you' and maintain the relationship with your clients than to have some sort of special event! Sometimes it takes more than just a thank you.

Ponies

One of my favorite people in the whole wide world lives in Northville, Michigan, near Detroit. Angela Carson is one of the top children's photographers in the country. We met many years ago in Las Vegas at a photography convention where Sue and I spoke. Over the years, we've bounced various marketing concepts back and forth to each other. Angela is a very giving person especially when it comes to her clients. She's very in to families and has a true passion for children. You can see the passion in the expressions of the children she photographs. The kids absolutely love her. Angela's way of giving back to her clients is by holding an "Angela Carson Photography Family Picnic."

Angela started this concept in 1994 and usually hosts around 300 of her clients, bringing in clowns, a petting zoo, and pony rides.

These 4 hour events are fully catered, allowing Angela the opportunity to maximize her socializing with clients and cost anywhere from $5-$7,000. Last year she even had the ice cream man show up in his truck and everyone got to choose their favorite ice cream. The picnic is held in a county park close to her studio that has a covered area just in case the weather doesn't cooperate. Clients receive their invitations about 6 weeks prior to the event. She believes that what sets her studio apart from her competition is the fact that she is truly focused on the family. Since parents are always looking for family activities, she's able to provide this special event and give a big thank you to her clients. Angela also mentioned that there is no immediate return for this type of marketing, but it is a great way to give back and she knows her clients look forward to and appreciate these events year after year.

More Ponies---Let's go to the races!

It's amazing how clients seem to surface in my life from time to time.

Every other year we hold the Sue Hudson Memorial Golf Tournament. A couple days prior to the event I received a call from a former high school senior client. "Hi, this is Stephanie Lorenz and you photographed my sister 10 years ago and me 18 years ago. I'm a realtor now and would love to sponsor a couple of holes at Sue's Golf Tourney."

"Sounds great," I said.

When Stephanie stopped by the next day to hand-deliver a check, she brought up the fact that I had just purchased the property adjacent to my studio. As we became reacquainted, I discovered that her real estate specialty was finding land for developers. Stephanie mentioned that I would probably be dealing with some annexation and zoning issues and that she would love to assist anyway she could. One of my long term business goals has always been to sell the studio property and eventually work from home, ultimately having enough business through existing clients (relationship marketing I have done over the years) to photograph, strictly on location, thus lower my overhead.

Through the next weeks and months I had the pleasure of getting to know this delightful lady is not your typical realtor, notable because she is very low key. When I mentioned I was writing a book on relationship marketing, Stephanie perked up and said, "Do you want to know how I say thanks to my clients each year? I take them to the race track! Do you want to come this summer?" Here is Stephanie's story.

As Stephanie put it so well, "it wasn't a day of business, it was a day for people to have a good time and relax." She couldn't have stated it any better. I say this with confidence because I had the opportunity to take part in her "Day at the Races."

Stephanie grew up with a genuine interest in horses and horse racing. She invited the majority of her clients she'd worked for during the last three years and all her active clients she's currently working for. I sensed this event wasn't just to say thanks for the business but a reflection of the way she actually does business, which is extremely detail oriented with class. Her mission was accomplished from the beginning with the letter her clients received mapping out the events of the day:

It's almost party time!

I've included your tickets for the Longacres Mile party on Sunday, Aug. 20. The admission ticket will get you into the grounds, one program/tip sheet, and buffet service so please hold on to your ticket until after lunch. I have also included a complimentary parking pass for convenient, reserved parking near the entrance.

Once inside the gates, the party tent is located trackside near the finish line. If you are facing the track, the tent will be to your right. (The horse owner's tent and our tent will be near each other so look for the Stephanie Lorenz banner.)

Please note Emerald Downs requires picture ID from everyone ordering alcoholic beverages… I have a fully hosted bar for your enjoyment so please remember to bring your ID!

First race at 1:00 — Buffet lunch around 3:00
Longacres Mile post time is approx. 4pm

I have sponsored one of the races! Let me know if you would like to be in the winner's circle (space is limited).

I'm looking forward to seeing you at the track on August 20!

Stephanie

THE RELATIONOGRAPHER

One of the things that I thought was masterful was the day she chose to have the event. How about the busiest day of the whole season? You could feel the excitement in the air!

Horse racing is very popular in the Seattle area. The first track was built in 1933 and was called Longacres. The biggest race of the year was always toward the end of the season in August, called the Longacres Mile. When the new track, Emerald Downs, replaced the old, the Longacres Mile still remained the title of the most prestigious race of the season. This was the day Steph chose for her event! Why that day? This is what's so masterful about her planning:

1) It's the most advertised and hyped racing day of the season. This reinforced the importance of being a part of something truly special, all compliments of Stephanie Lorenzo Realty. She was able to ride the marketing coat tails of Emerald Downs without paying a penny for it.

2) All the extra goodies, such as pony rides, face painting, etc., were free to everyone at the track that day!

While Stephanie was able to save money on these 2 items, she definitely made up for it everywhere else! As my son, Josh, and I entered one of the entrance gates from our preferred parking space (she had included), you could feel the buzz of the crowd. As we tried to make our way through the crowd to find Stephanie's private tent we noticed other private parties going on. We asked for directions and got, "I think it's the big tent down by the finish line!" They were right! Settled next to the Longacre Mile owner's little tent was Stephanie's much larger, very impressive tent complex! It was a very warm day in Seattle (in the 90's, very hot for us Northwest people) so having the extra shade came in handy!

Let the party begin! On the tables were racing forms, programs, tip sheets, and some of Stephanie's goodies, including little toys for the kids and real estate information for the adults. Thirsty—oh yes! Open bar, oh yes! A little hungry—yep! Great hors d'oeuvres. Ok, let's start picking some winners. After Josh and I chose our respective horse for the 1st race, we walked up to Stephanie's personnel ticket booth. As we made our way up there we were intercepted by Stephanie, "Here's a $2 voucher on me!" Wow! That $2 coupon was worth 100 times its value with everything else we had experienced in the last hour!

Josh's horse beat my horse that race but there's always the next race, right? As we thumbed through the race program to see all of our future financial opportunities, I spotted that Stephanie had sponsored the fifth race. I'm thinking, as a fellow business owner, what does that cost? It didn't matter, as it was extremely impressive. As the horses were entering the starting gate for the fifth race, there was a sense of camaraderie under the tent. It wasn't just Stephanie's race, but all of ours.

When discussing her event later for this book, Stephanie hit a bull's eye, "There is no better form of marketing then having people identify with you. Events are like an extension of you and your business."

During the fifth race, many of Stephanie's clients made their way down to the finish line and into the winner's circle for pictures with Stephanie, the winning horse and its owners. Once again, a great example of how to identify with a brand or company.

As Josh and I left the Day at the Races, we felt we were special. Stephanie believes that, "If you're in a business where people don't want to be made to feel special, you should get into a different business. I don't know anyone who doesn't like to feel special. I would love to go to a party that has preferred parking, free drinks, lots of food and lots of fun."

The realty profession is not easy. With so many realtors competing and the trend to sell homes on your own, loyalty is rare. Stephanie feels, "There's no substitute for loyalty; you can't buy loyalty. If you cultivate relationships with people you respect and they have respect for what you do, you just can't NOT be loyal."

It's amazing what you learn from the people around you, even a former high school senior portrait client. Stephanie's memorable event was a perfect example of taking "saying thank you" to a new level, not only to her clients, but her prospective clients too! You know that there wasn't one person that attended the event that didn't mention it to someone at work Monday morning! I sure did!

Popcorn

Another realtor, Cheri Lang, one of my many clients who are realtors, recently sold my house for me, and while the house was on the market, I was privileged to receive her marketing pieces. She does a great job of keeping in touch with her clients, even *after* the sale! I have to share one of her ideas that caught my attention.

Keeping in touch with past clients is one thing, but stepping up and taking action is quite another. Cheri has done this by hosting a movie night for her past "A" list clients. The first year, about 175 people attended, and last year she nearly doubled that number due to enjoyment had by all. This movie party takes place near Thanksgiving, in light of the "giving thanks" theme, and since many of her clients are families, it fits in nicely with upcoming fun holiday movies.

Cheri begins by contacting the theater to reserve her date and time and then produces an invitation that is sent out to her top clients. Because snacks are a must while at the movies, snack vouchers are given to clients as they walk through the door. At the beginning of the movie she presents her team of employees while she personally thanks everyone for attending and being her loyal clients. At the end of the movie she does the same, once again thanking everyone for attending and for future referrals. Cheri enjoys this type of giving back because in her words, "it's very clean," meaning her and her staff effortlessly show up, graciously host, and everyone leaves happy.

Cheri's relationship marketing ideas come from a variety of people with various theories. Rather than compiling a large list to manage and maintain in her data base, she constantly updates and focuses on the people "you're really going to have a relationship with. When you start out with a list of 1,000 people, you can't be real about it." So Cheri really narrows down her clients to the people she wants to stay in touch with on a monthly basis. Whether through her monthly newsletter, mouse pads, or scratch pads with her logo, her point is to constantly stay in touch.

Cheri has done this very well with the majority of high end listings in our community. Her goal is to have the community think of her when they think of high-end real estate, thus she is branding herself. The movie night is just one of many ways she's able to promote her brand to her existing clients. Like any realtor, future business depends on referrals from people she has made a positive impression on.

Pinots

I love to socialize with my clients… dinner, parties, golf, maybe even a little wine tasting. The only problem is that I have so many incredible clients and such limited time to spend with them. So why not plan a combined dinner with multiple couples? Ok, let's do it! The first thing to plan is the location. Next is the caterer. Then who do you invite? What kind of activities could we do?

My goals for the evening were to:
- Make it a unique experience
- Make it fun and memorable
- Make it personalized
- Make it a big 'thank you' from me, my staff, and my family

Making it unique

The location I chose for the evening helped with this. Glass art is big in the Pacific Northwest, especially in Seattle. This is because the famous glass artist Dale Chihuly lives here and occasionally gives workshops.

Down the hill from my business, there's a glass blowing studio and antique store called Uptown Glassworks, owned by a fellow Renton Rotarian. During one of our weekly luncheon meetings, I had the opportunity to sit next to him when he casually mentioned that he was starting to rent out his facility for wedding rehearsal dinners, corporate parties, and other special events. The rental fee even included a team of glass blowing artists that would provide the entertainment by creating a beautiful piece of art that evening, very unique and just what I was looking for!

Having the client dinner at this location also helped determine how many couples we would invite. It comfortably held fifty– so the number of couples worked out to be 25. This was exactly what I had planned for in the budget. The invitations read:

Sometimes just saying "Thank You" isn't enough..."

All of us at Hudson's would like to say thanks for the opportunity to photograph you this past year. Sometimes just saying thanks isn't enough!

This is one of those times.

You're invited to a very special evening dedicated to you! We've chosen a unique location, Uptown Glassworks in Renton. Several of their artists will be featured that evening creating glass art. Appetizers and dinner will be provided by the Melrose Grill and Armondo's Italian Café, with wines for tasting too. Jeremy Ryan, composer/pianist/recording artist, will entertain us with his talents.

The date for this event is:

Friday, February 4th

6:30pm

Uptown Glassworks
230 Main Avenue South
Renton, WA

We would be honored by your presence.
Please RSVP by January 15th.
425-271-9709 • 800-952-6609 • brucehudson@earthlink.net

We look forward to having you as our guests!

Bruce and the staff at Hudson's

PONIES, POPCORN, AND PINOTS

Now the hard part… who do you invite? As I mentioned before, I have the best job in the world and I also have the best clients in the world! How could we pick just 25 couples? I knew that if this dinner was a success, I would maybe have one or two a year. So if a couple wasn't invited this time, they would be in the future. I wanted a good cross section of clients– wedding, family, and children's portraits. I also wanted some twenty-plus year clients, brand new clients, and everything in between. So with the help of my staff, I came up with a list of forty or so couples.

My office manager Debbie came up with the great idea of calling the couples before sending the formal invitations. Many of the couples unfortunately couldn't make it to our dinner, but were still honored that we thought of them.

Now that we had the location and the RSVP's rolling in, we moved on to our next goal.

Making it fun and memorable

I have a buddy that owns and operates two very fine restaurants, an Italian gem called "Armondo's," and his newest, "The Melrose," that's an incredible steak place. As you might recall, I featured him in *Keeping in Touch*. We're constantly sharing marketing ideas back and forth for our respective businesses.

When I mentioned to Mondo about catering and the concept of the evening, he got visibly excited! "How about doing some wine tasting," he suggested, "I'll talk to one of my wine reps." That sounds like fun– wine tasting before and during dinner, while watching the glass blowing. This party was starting to come together nicely!

One neat thing that Uptown Glassworks has been doing the last few years is getting the general public involved in blowing glass. At Christmas, you can make your own ornament. At Halloween, its pumpkins, and during our client dinner in early February, it was hearts. For a nominal fee, my clients had the opportunity to blow their own glass heart paperweights. What a great way to create something memorable to remember the evening by!

Making it personalized

I love telling the story of my clients through the art of portraits. Each client is so unique and the dynamics of each session so different. This part of my job is the most challenging, yet most rewarding. Personalizing every image is what I try to achieve day in and day out and I wanted to add this personalization to this special evening– but how?

When ordering, all of my clients get to see their images via a slide show, set to music. Up until a few years ago, the equipment consisted of two simple carousel slide projectors with a dissolver unit to blend the images together back and forth. It worked great. Today, with the new technology, I use a digital projector and laptop computer to achieve the same result. How about having a little surprise presentation, featuring each of my clients in attendance? What a perfect fit. I already had all of the images from their most recent sessions, and I also knew (because of all the RSVP's) exactly who was going to be there that evening. So I put together a personalized show for the evening. In some cases, I was able to include multiple images of each client on one slide. I also added text on each slide, such as "The Jones Family" or "Dick and Jane's wedding." In addition, during the actual show I played some music that helped create an uplifting mood. All in all, the presentation was a huge success. I observed many tears in the audience, some of which came from seeing their own images, but I actually observed the most emotion from the moving collection of images of their fellow diners.

A Big Thank You

Sometimes just saying thank you isn't enough. One of the most pleasurable parts of the evening was the opportunity to personally serve our clients. Mondo and his team of chefs beautifully plated each dinner, but it was my staff and my family who actually served at the table. The food was fabulous, but the reaction from our clients was the highlight of the evening. Just the heartfelt look in their eye as we delivered the meal signaled, "Mission accomplished!"

Another way we made the evening fun and memorable was a couple of surprise gifts. They weren't lavish or expensive, just another little 'thanks for being with us tonight,' and thank you for being a client. As our guests arrived, we greeted them at the entrance of Uptown Glassworks. We presented a beautiful long stemmed rose to each of the ladies as they arrived. None of my clients had ever been to the glassworks, so I was curious to see their reaction. Uptown's is a cross between a "funky" old antique store and a working glass blowing studio. My clients reacted with, "Wow, what a cool place, I didn't realize this place existed."

The second gift was handed out at the end of the evening as our couples were leaving. I'm sure you're aware of the coffee and espresso craze in the Northwest, and particularly in the Seattle area. A former client/student, Brett Habenicht, began his own espresso shop, Java Java Coffee Company (to be mentioned in further detail in *Relationship Masters*). It's wonderful coffee and that's what we served for our special evening. For years we've used Java Java coffee in a half-pound bag as a small 'thank you' for my clients. Brett has allowed us to attach our own custom labels to the bag, making it proudly "Hudson's Designer Roast", mentioned in the chapter *It's the Little Things*. This is what we handed out to everyone as they left. It's what they enjoyed at dinner and now it's what they can enjoy at home. Hopefully they'll think of Hudson's and the evening they spent with us as they're enjoying it.

In any business or service, sometimes just saying thank you is not enough. Building a relationship, as we've discussed in this book, is essential and maintaining it is critical. If you're able to take your thank you's "up a couple of notches", you'll guarantee your special relationship with your client or customer for the life of your business. It's the type of marketing dollars I love to spend and best of all, having events with ponies, popcorn, or pinots is just plain fun!

9

WIN-WIN MARKETING:
Relationship Marketing to the Masses

This chapter goes a little "against the grain" compared to the rest of the book. Relationship marketing is based on keeping in touch with existing clients/customers. When I say going against the grain, I mean in some cases the people that this form of marketing effort reaches, might not be customers or clients *yet*. I'm going to be referring to different companies and organizations that like to keep in touch, but like to keep in touch with the masses. Most marketing experts call this Institutional Advertising. Everybody knows who McDonald's is because they continue to advertise on a huge scale. The ads we see repeatedly for a new kid's meal, toy, or sandwich bring awareness to that particular new product. But for the most part McDonalds ads are institutionalized where it's based on "Hey, we're still here, we're McDonalds! Stop by and check out our newest thing!"

This form of relationship marketing to the masses takes on a different twist when you have businesses not just blitzing the masses with advertising but sponsoring various events or venues. I like to call this *Win-Win Marketing*. The company or business sponsoring the event is rewarded because of the recognition they receive, and the organization that hosts the event also wins through the financial contribution of the sponsor. We've been very successful with this win-win marketing concept in our local area over the years. Many cities, big and small, have community celebrations. We have Renton River Days. During that week in July there are many special events, including an evening jazz concert that we've sponsored. The size, style and cost to sponsor the event fits well with a business my size.

The concert takes place in our new town square, the Piazza and it's the perfect venue for this kind of performance. The organizers of the event knew of my background in jazz and asked if we would like to sponsor the event. The answer was, "Absolutely!" We got numerous name mentions and name recognition in the various promotional marketing pieces and in the newspaper. The concert took place on a beautiful July evening. We created a colorful 16 foot banner that was strung across the stage which had "Jazz at the Piazza" logo as well as our Hudson logo. We set up display portraits that were 30x40 inch framed canvas. We displayed them around the piazza area with a couple of tables with more examples of our wedding albums, senior portraits, and family portraits. We also brought brochures to promote each type of photography we offer. It was an extremely warm evening for our area (ninety degrees), we also brought a big tub of our "Hudson Water Bottles" to give out. It proved to be a huge hit! As the people arrived at the concert, they were able to stroll around and see our work as they listened to some great jazz. This event has become a tradition. It's amazing to see how many people would come up, either during or after the concert, and be truly grateful for our participation and our sponsorship in putting this concert together. This type of "win-win" marketing proves that even though there may not be an immediate return on investment (I did not sign up perspective clients at the concert), it clearly demonstrated that we like to give back to the community, and that we provide some unique opportunities. We are proud to be a part of our community and support this event in a way that fits our budget. Once again it's a win-win for everyone.

During the last 20 years of Renton River Days, my attorney, Dan Kellogg, who handles all of my family law, sponsors the senior citizen picnic. Dan specializes in estate planning so you can see how this is the perfect opportunity to get his name out in front of his target market. He's sponsored this picnic since the beginning and it's an annual event that he looks forward to providing. It's also a part of his annual budget and beleives it's very cost effective. What relates nicely with Dan's annual picnic is his Pro-Bono clinic. He does a monthly free seminar at the Senior Citizens Center. It covers a broad range of things and it's designed to make Dan available to people who can't afford a lawyer. He meets with six clients in a half hour setting. Dan guesses that maybe a 1/3 or half the seniors at the seminar wouldn't really have the ability to afford to see a lawyer.

It's a win-win situation. Dan adds tremendous value to the programs at the Senior Center and it's meeting a valuable need in the community. He hopes that his name is the one that comes to mind when people are looking for a lawyer. In talking with many seniors in the community, they have heard of Dan and his contributions. It's working!

Everyone who comes to the picnic pays a dollar so they'll have a vested interest in attending. Seniors tend to pinch their pennies and when they pay for something they want to enjoy the benefits. Luckily it's not such a large amount that really is a barrier to anyone. Dan, in addition to the Senior Center, pays roughly $1,200 for food and entertainment. They usually have the Renton City Concert band come in and play before the picnic followed by dancing. "As you know, this type of marketing is really a long-range proposition so there aren't really any tangible results. You have to stay with it, repeatedly." Dan doesn't do this primarily for business, but as a public service instead. As he puts it so well, "It certainly does provide a good vibe on the street." Every now and then someone will come and say that they enjoyed the picnic last year and they look forward to it next year. So obviously people are aware of it and that's a good thing. It's a wonderful event for the seniors and it's a great way to invite them to Renton River days with an affordable picnic. Because they love it and have a good time it does good things for Dan's law firm, reinforcing that he and his staff support the senior community.

The City of Renton has been very proactive in attracting all types of new businesses. They figured this out after 9/11 when airplane sales at Boeing started to decline. The main Boeing factory is located in Renton where they make the most popular commercial plane, the 737. Alone, the Renton plant actually produces 42% of the world's commercially flown aircraft. More than one thousand 737's have been delivered around the world from our city's facility.1 When 9/11 happened the airline business tanked, and so did Boeing. It was about that time when the city of Renton became more proactive in attracting commerce than the typical red tape-jump-through-hoops bureaucracy that most city governments exhibit. One of the companies they were able to attract to our area was Ikea. From the very beginning of Ikea being a part of our community they recognized the importance of truly giving back to the community. I had the opportunity to meet and get to know one of the partners of Ikea, Bjorn, while he and I served on our Renton Chamber of Commerce Board of Directors. Later, through some photography I did with both owners, I had the opportunity to meet partner #2, Anders. If you have never been to an Ikea store, you're in for a big treat. They have stores all over the world stocked with everything you can imagine for your home, business, or garden. This Swedish-based company is huge with very affordable merchandise. Their slogan quite simply is "To shop at Ikea, you don't have to be rich—just smart!" Both of my kid's apartments in college were outfitted solely by Ikea products. And best of all it fit in an SUV! (Of course, some assembly required.)

The Renton Ikea is a little different than its fellow Ikea stores around the world. Most Ikea's are corporate owned, but the Renton store is owner and corporate combined. In fact, it was an experiment to see if owner operated stores could run as well or better than solely corporate stories. The result was astounding, with sales having surged from $25 million in the first 10 months of the store opening to over

$137 million in 2005. In 2004 they had their first $3 million dollar day. The Renton Ikea even has its own restaurant where they've sold, to date, over 25 million Swedish meatballs!

When Bjorn and Anders went into business together they wanted to share any success with their staff and their community. I found one of their comments very interesting, "Since we've arrived in North America in 1997, we've noticed that the culture of giving is stronger in North America than in any other country we've seen, even in our homeland of Sweden, where the community is taken care of by the government."

They didn't really have a set plan or budget for community support, but knew they wanted to step up as "opportunities come and go." In 2003 one of those opportunities surfaced in a big way!

Our oldest high school in the Renton area really needed a face lift a few years ago. It's a beautiful brick building but needed a lot of restoration so the community rallied around the school district and approved bond issues and levies to go ahead and restore Renton High School. During that time the Renton School District decided to also renovate the auditorium, which really needed a lot of work. The architects and some of the main players of the project suggested that the school district might want to partner with the city and the community at large to create a performing arts center. The price tag on this was roughly 1.5 million dollars and so the leaders of our city formed a committee to raise the money needed. These were going to be funds that were outside what the school district had already purposed. So this truly was going to be a performing arts center that would serve the community.

Within a years time the committee got to the point where they felt good about the amount of money they had raised to make this dream a reality. But they were still in need of $500,000. At first they weren't really looking for one big contributor for the huge sum, but when they got very close to having enough money and just needed one big donation, someone in the committee approached Ikea. It was the opportunity that Bjorn and Anders had been looking for and with a generous $500,000 donation to the cause, Ikea made the entire project possible. It was the type of circumstance where everything came together perfectly. Truely a win-win situation. Surprisingly Bjorn and Anders were not exactly sure if their corporate partners knew about the investment, "our President of North American stores actually read it in the papers that we were giving away a half million dollars!" After the news broke, Bjorn received a phone call asking what this was all about. "It was hard to tell corporate; you can't calculate certain things in business and marketing, sometimes they just fit the mold to what is right and you want to do it!"

Today, despite what Ikea corporate, Bjorn, and Anders discussed, the Ikea Performing Arts Center is one of the shining stars of our community. Our local Ikea consistently boasts the largest sale volume in North America! Wow! It's obviously been a win-win for everyone!

On a smaller scale, that performing arts committee contacted businesses and private citizens to also ask for donations. My studio was able to contribute at a lower level, but we still got the same valuable name recognition. If you go into the lobby of this performing arts center today you're able to see gold, silver or platinum stars that are imbedded in the floor with the name or business that contributed to that particular level. It's remarkable to see the name of our business there on the floor in a star. For us it was a one time investment, but it's given us a greater longevity in contributing to our community and the building of this wonderful performing arts center.

Every year the performing arts center produces a series of concerts and events, an every year the quality of performers and performances improves. With every event there is the opportunity to be a sponsor. The price tag to sponsor fits the budget of a small business like ours. How do you justify your investment in this type of win-win marketing? Once again, there's no immediate return on investment. Most marketing gurus would say this is a stupid way to use your marketing dollars! I totally disagree!

The first time we sponsored an event at the performing arts

center, the director, Shana Pennington-Baird, was able to partner with the Seattle FM Jazz Station for pennies on the dollar! For one week before the event, this station played a spot for the concert every hour on the hour! I was unaware of this until numerous clients of mine, during the week called, emailed and mentioned, "I liked your commercial on KWJZ."

"What commercial are you talking about?" I asked. "The one about that performance you're sponsoring at the Renton Performing Arts Center on Friday!" In most cases my clients didn't recall the event, just the fact that we were the business to sponsor it! To me, that's a win-win! Good for the community, good for us.

Most recently, in this years concert series we had the opportunity to sponsor a musician that I consider a genius and composer at piano, George Winston. You might have heard of him through the years with some of his CD's classics, Dec, Winter, Autumn. He's kind of a "New Age" type of musician that was popular before the New Age Movement started.

As we had done with the jazz concert at the Piazza and other performing arts center events, we took full advantage and displayed our work in large canvas portraits and albums. Shana, the director, had no problem with giving us space throughout the lobby for framed portraits on easels with lights and tables for albums and brochures. Two weeks before the Winston concert, Shana called me and said, "Do you realize that we only have 20 seats left for the concert! We've never had a sell-out in the history of the theater. Would you mind sending out one of your e-newsletters to your clients?" It took about 30 minutes or so to prepare and send the e-marketing piece, but only 5 minutes before Shana started receiving calls for tickets. The concert ended up being a huge success and sell-out with even a waiting list the day of the event! As Mr. Winston started his performance to a packed house, it was extremely gratifying to know that we had been a major part of making it happen. The audience was filled with many of my clients and future clients. From the thanks we received during the intermission and days after the concert, everyone enjoyed the concert and appreciated our sponsorship! Win-win marketing is about building relationships with the masses. For us that night the masses numbered about 340. For businesses like the Renton Ikea the masses can be in the millions throughout the Puget Sound region!

Ikea is in a unique position like many large businesses that want to maintain a connection with customers but find it more challenging to do with the immense number of customers they cater too. The owners of the Renton Ikea have worked hard to make Ikea a household name through advertising on TV while also showing a strong commitment to community support. Anders stated, "When you're speaking of community, yes, our involvement has helped us with our sales." As a member of the community, I see Ikea's presence as vastly improving the quality of life for everyone in the area. Not just its customers, but for the general public, some that have never stepped foot into Ikea...yet!

The list of sponsorships and commitments that Ikea provides my Renton community is huge. Most of our major chamber of commerce events have Ikea involved one way or another. They work with Junior Achievement, the University of Washington, and countless other organizations. Ikea has found that to market to its core customers effectively, it needs to also market to everyone in the area. Yes, they do mass mailings of their catalogue to over a million, but they also choose a style of relationship marking where everyone wins! Our Renton area is fortunate to have Bjorn, Anders, and their amazing store. It's truly a win-win scenario with our community benefiting as well as the largest grossing Ikea in North America. The "win-win" combination is an obvious success!

"Win-win" marketing can come in many shapes and sizes, especially when it comes to the size of the business and budget. There's many ways to maintain a relationship even to future clients or customers. It could be sponsoring a golf hole for a charity tournament or donating for the naming rights of a performing arts center; "win-win" marketing might not give you an instant return on investment but certainly increases your position in the community. It is truly a "win-win" for everyone!

---

[1] Boeing, "Boeing Commercial Airplanes 737 Manufacturing Site: Renton, WA," Commercial Airplanes (accessed April 11, 2006).

10

PERFORMING LIKE A ROCK STAR!

Keep customers/clients coming back with consistent passion and a high level of performance

As you read in the introduction of this book, I used to be a high school band director. Although my teaching career only lasted 4 years, it changed my life forever. I learned a lot about life teaching music to junior high and high school students. I learned never to give them examples of what I might have done when I was in junior high. A few weeks into my first year I bragged about the time in seventh grade when we had a substitute fill in for my instructor and we would switch instruments. When the substitute tried to have us play one of our pieces of music it sounded terrible. You can image how it sounded as all havoc broke out! Sure enough, some 10 years later, the first time I called a substitute in, guess what my wonderful seventh graders did? You guessed it; they switched their instruments and created havoc for *my* substitute to the point where she vowed she would never substitute for me again, live and learn I guess. Maybe that is why I only taught 4 years?

Along those lines, I feel as though I missed out on a lot of good music from, the late 70s and early 80s, mainly because I was so focused on trying to teach junior high and high school students what I thought was better music at the time. I had concert, jazz band, and marching band, all the typical bands of junior and high school. In the morning I would get to school early and put on music I thought would add culture to their lives, but all they wanted to listen to was Sting, Foreigner, Boston and Styx. I knew of that music, but I didn't really learn to love it. And so, in recent years I've had the opportunity to go and see some of these bands (although it's 25 years later). I have a former band student Brad that has become a really good friend of mine (which is really strange because I first met him when he was in eighth grade). Who would have thought 25 years later he would be a close friend and now be educating me to appreciate music? At the ripe old age of 38, Brad got married to Danielle (another client of mine I photographed as a high school senior in 1987) and I had the opportunity to photograph their wedding. Right after he proposed to her on a beach just south of Newport, Oregon, which included Danielle finding a ring in an oyster shell, he immediately proclaimed he knew who was going to do the wedding photography. But she said *she* knew who would do the pictures. Lucky for me, they *both* wanted me to photograph their wedding! This is the kind of story I love to hear.

As I have preached throughout this book, business is all about relationships. Here is a wonderful example of two separate client relationships that were created some 20 years apart, but yet extremely powerful. Both relationships created a desire to have me work with them when it came down to photographing one of the most important days of their lives!

The Pacific Northwest in general and the Seattle area in particular have always been a part of the music scenes cutting edge. In the late 60s and early 70s we had Jimmy Hendrix, and more recently Nirvana, Green Day, Pearl Jam, and Dave Matthew's Band. But one group in particular that has been around forever also came from this area, the 1970's rock group Heart. This is one of those weird situations where I've been familiar with the songs of Heart but never realized that Heart was the band performing them. Basically, I have always been a Heart fan and just never knew it! One of Brad and Danielle's hobbies and passions is seeking out and going to rock concerts. Brad is a master at finding the best seats when tickets become available. If you view one of Heart's recent performance DVDs, you'll see Brad a number of times in the front row handing roses to both Nancy and Ann Wilson.

The past few years I've had the opportunity to go to some of these concerts thanks to Brad and Danielle and experienced their killer seats. I actually got to see Heart for the first time, in person, front row, right below stage within inches of these artists. It was really inspiring! These incredible ladies are in their mid 50s, and they play with as much soul, heart (no pun), and passion as they did when they started 25 years ago.

I feel relationship marketing comes with a consistent level of performance and passion. What do I mean by that? Where did that come from? Heart gives a performance many years ago, the fans buy their records (my God, I'm really dating myself), they enjoy them, and the fans keep coming back when they're in town 5, 10, 15, 20 years later! The continued high level of performance and pride that some of these artists exhibit exemplifies a great way to maintain the relationship they have with their fans/customers. Sure, we all have a connection to certain performers and their music. We've all had a favorite song or album (dating myself again) at one point in our life that stirs profound memories or feelings each time we hear it. What song or group had the most impact on your life growing up? What song takes you back to where you originally first heard it?

"American Pie," 1972! My junior year (Sue's senior year) was an amazing time in my life. I was passionate about everything (maybe that was my hormones running crazy)! I was a member of one of the top high school jazz bands in the country. Every time we competed we won! We were rock stars—well, in a high school jazz band kind of way. I had a hot senior cheerleader that was my first love and girlfriend. I found that I was pretty good at photography, a hobby I really enjoyed. Many an hour was spent in the darkroom, developing and printing images for the high school yearbook, newspaper, and friends, and I was getting paid for it! Many of those long hours were spent listening to the radio and the popular songs of the day. American Pie was one of those songs that played all the time. Still to this day, the moment I hear the first few bars, "A long, long, time ago," it takes me back to 1972 and being on top of the world (so to speak).

Another performer that I've never really appreciated is Elton John. I've heard his songs throughout the years but I never really listened to them. My lady, Terri has been a huge fan for years and has seen Elton 4 times in concert. A couple of years ago I got Terri a collection of his live concerts on DVD. Recently we sat down one evening with a glass of wine (okay, a few glasses) and started to watch Elton in concert. As my mind opened to this incredible performer my ears began to listen to the words and not just the music. In a matter of a couple hours, I became Elton's newest fan. Ironically, a couple days later Brad and Danielle called to ask if Terri and I wanted to go see Elton John. If they had asked a month sooner I would have not been all that excited, but after my recent inoculation I was ecstatic to experience Elton in person!

Because of Elton's popularity in Seattle, his first show sold out instantly. Fortunately for us, they decided to add a second show. That's the one we went to on a Saturday night. The reviews from the Friday show were exceptional which made the excitement for Saturday's concert even more heightened. As we arrived at our seats, the buzz in the room was something I had never experience before. The excitement from everyone around me was contagious.

The place just exploded when they introduced Elton John. Throughout the concert, Elton put his heart and soul into every word and note on the piano with a passion I had never witnessed in any other performer. This level of performance connected with everyone in attendance. One of the things that impressed me the most was his humility. Someone with his fame and fortune could easily be a real jerk, but he was just the opposite. Elton's response from thousands of his fans after each song he played was as sincere as he was truly grateful for being there entertaining his faithful followers. Time just flew by that night as everyone became mesmerized by this legend. As Elton John returned for his encore, security allowed what looked to be VIPs up to the stage. They were all holding memorabilia from hats to old albums. Elton made his way across the stage and started to personally greet his fans. He signed each and every piece of memorabilia. I mean everyone's, not just the fans in front, but six rows deep. This display of mutual respect and affection lasted some 15-20 minutes, all the time the crowd maintained a roaring standing ovation! No wonder this amazing artist has had a four decade following!

Without a doubt this was the best concert I've experienced. It put all the elements together that I feel are important to continue and maintain long lasting relationships. Whether you're a rock star or business owner, these elements should be demonstrated with every performance.

Triad of Performance

The term triad in music means three separate tones that create a chord. All these are needed to produce a harmonic message. I feel it's the same with maintaining a high level performance. There are 3 elements needed, the 1st is talent.

Talent: this is such a subjective term but in order to achieve a high level of performance that will stand out from the rest, you need talent. We all know people, performers, and businesses that may display just a moderate amount of talent but have much success in what they do. On the flip side I'm sure we all know extremely talented people who have never come close to rising to the level of success they deserve. Why is that? It takes more than talent to be successful.

Passion: the second element in this triad of performance is passion. Throughout my music career I was somewhat talented. Many of my fellow trumpet players were much more talented than me. What helped me was my consistency and passion for the instrument. I was fortunate growing up to have some of the best trumpet teachers in the

THE RELATIONOGRAPHER

Seattle area. My last teacher was Bill Cole at Western Washington University in Bellingham, Washington. He was a wonderful instructor and a great human being. He was the one who gave me the opportunity to play with Bob Hope the summer of 1978. He was supposed to play the gig but wasn't feeling up to it because of some cancer treatments, so he asked me if I wanted to do it. The show was slated for 7 p.m. with the rehearsal at 2 p.m. The conductor quickly put all of us at ease with his humor and quick wit, "For most of you, playing tonight for Mr. Hope will be a once in a lifetime adventure. Just play your hearts out and enjoy the ride."

"Where's Mr. Hope?" asked the lead alto sax player.

"He's where he's always at this time of day...on a golf course somewhere. He'll probably get 27, maybe even 36 holes in today. There's a good chance the show won't be starting on time tonight, so like I said before, just enjoy the ride!"

As the rehearsal progressed, it really hit me that I was reading and playing music that was part of history. This "book"[2] had been all over the world for who knows how many U.S.O. tours and countless shows! We finished the rehearsal about 4 p.m. and then went to get a bite to eat. Upon returning to the arena we noticed how bad the traffic had backed up. Seven o'clock turned into 8 p.m., still no Bob Hope. Finally about 8:15 p.m. we got our cue to start the show. From all indications, Mr. Hope did get all 36 holes of golf in that day. If I had told you I wasn't just a little nervous, I'd be lying. He was amazing! Each joke was better than the last and all related to the local area and culture. He had been briefed in the limo on the way back from the golf course by his writers. Even more astounding was that he never used any cue cards! One of the things I admired most was his timing and delivery. He had an amazing passion for entertaining the crowd. That level of passion and tremendous talent elevated his performance to a world class level. To have the opportunity to witness his greatness impresses me to this day.

That summer had many highs for me, playing for Bob Hope and

graduating from WWU, but there was one major low for me, the loss of my instructor Bill Cole. His cancer moved rapidly, and he was gone before any of the treatments took hold. Bill was the one who taught me to play with passion, "There are trumpet players, and there are musicians that play trumpet. It's the musicians who get the gigs", he told me. "Anyone can learn to play the music, but it's a musician that has the ability to feel the music." You're telling a story. You're job is to evoke emotions from the listener so that they feel the same interpretation that you're feeling. Bill taught me to search from the inside and find that place which contains your soul. "Passion resides in your soul! Everyone has passion, but few rarely know where it resides." What an incredible life lesson to be cherished and used on a daily basis. Thank you Bill Cole!

Consistency: I touched on this in the first chapter, but after my "Elton Experience" it takes on a greater dimension. Before, during, and even after the concert I was constantly reminded by all his fans of how Elton always puts on a great concert. I mentioned before this was Terri's 5th time seeing him perform and according to her, this performance lived up to all the others…phenomenal! As a consumer it's nice to have those expectations met, or better yet, exceeded. I'm sure you'll agree that a McDonald's hamburger isn't the best tasting burger you've ever eaten, but it's probably the most consistent tasting from city to city. Part of building relationships is a matter of trust, that is trusting you're going to receive the same level performance consistently! As a consumer you're always going to compare a product or service with the last experience you had.

So let's review a bit shall we? World class performers have an ability to maintain a connection with their fans for decades. A great form of relationship marketing. To perform like a rock star you need the Triad of Performance: talent, consistency, and passion. The more of each of these you possess and utilize the better chance you have to perform like a rock star and continue to have fans throughout the years!

How does this relate to my business of photography? Well, after photographing professionally some 25 years, you'd think I'd be tired of it, but I'm really not. It's been delightful the past few months having my son Josh working at the studio. We're getting ready to move out of our facility into a new home, on beautiful Lake Sawyer on the foothills of the Cascade Mountains. This home has been designed as a retreat for my family and hopefully many grand kids. But my business will also be at this location. Because of all the relationship marketing techniques I have shared with you in these pages and the implementation of these concepts the past 25 years, I am now at the point in my career where 95% of my business will come from existing clients. Twenty-five years of photography has created an enormous amount of film negatives and recently, digital negatives. I've always had a hard time deciding what to keep for my clients and what to throw out. One of Josh's jobs has been to identify and keep only the negatives/files clients purchase and to throw out all the rest. Here's a kid that grew up in the photography business, but never really sat down and realized the amount, and hopefully the quality of work, I've created the last twenty-five years. As he goes through these files one by one, it's fun to have him exclaim, "Wow, Dad! You've been doing this a long time! How do you stay so consistent? I don't know how you do it." Creating a high level of performance for your clients so they continue to come back time and time again, much like the fans of rock stars I mentioned before, is a huge part of maintaining the relationship,.

Quality restaurants must have it the hardest. Their consistency day in and day out is what keeps their patrons loyal. Every time I step behind a camera my goal is to capture the essence of the subject I'm photographing. When I wake up each Saturday (most weddings are on Saturdays) I prepare for the importance of the day. "I'm going to be photographing a couple's wedding and I need to be at my best. These are images they are going to cherish forever." Their kids, grandkids, and great-grandkids are going to fight over the images in the future. No pressure at all! When I consider the level of responsibility I have for my clients, it helps me raise the level of my performance and inject passion in what I do. Producing images that will be enjoyed for many generations! May all those images rock on!

---

[2] Slang term for a collection of music.

11

RELATIONSHIP MASTERS

This final chapter is a culmination of everything that I have shared with you so far about relationship marketing. As mentioned continually throughout this book, most of my ideas have come from outside the photography industry. In fact many have come from my clients. I don't think that any of these ideas are earth shatteringly new, but more importantly, the people that have implemented these ideas in their businesses have done it masterfully. That is why I call them relationship masters! Enjoy.

Hudson Designer Portraits
7 steps to better photography

Hey that's me! I thought I'd get the ball rolling with this example. I love to teach and share ideas. I especially love to share ideas with my clients. Years ago I had a conversation with a client of mine at the studio who was talking about going on vacation and inquiring as to what kind of camera they should buy. What should they do? With all the teaching I do for professional photographers, it was fun helping the non-professionals take better vacation photographs. At the end of the conversation the client mentioned that I should put on photography classes for my clients. I was thinking, "Would I be training my competition, or creating new photographers to become my competition?" They might get good enough and end up not coming to me. That was a stupid thought. I've been doing this a long time and people enjoy the images I create. Having a *Client Camera Class* would be a good way to keep in touch with the clients. It's a win-win because the client learns a little more about photography, and they would possibly grow to appreciate what I do that much more.

We started having very successful Client Camera Classes. We let our clients know the date for a class through our newsletter, and it would instantly be filled. We try to limit the number of students to about 20-25 so there is better intimacy, thus making the class a lot more fun. The last few times I've held the classes we've had an admission charge of a couple bags of groceries to be donated to the local food bank. With the bag of groceries, it tends to fill our lobby when they come, which is great. It's been fun to see people come with their cameras, camera bags, and unopened manuals they were asked to bring. We talk about things like exposure, lighting, posing, and my favorite, what you can do to make people look better! I've modified this to a program that I give to Kiwanis clubs, Rotary clubs, and Soroptimists called *7 Steps to Better Photography*. It's just some quick and easy tips that will instantly improve their work, whether it's during the holidays or on vacation, as it seems everyone wants to improve their photography skills. I can't tell you how many times our efforts resulted in thank you cards and calls which expressed how nice it was of us to help them become better photographers. For my business, sharing information and having a camera class is an inexpensive way give back to our clients and to maintain that relationship with them.

Paolo's Italian Restaurant
Sharing the passion for cooking

Another of my favorite local restaurants is Paolo's (for some reason food and wine is woven into this book). I've known the owner and chef, Paul Raftis for many years, having grown up with him and gone to the same high school. Since he was a little kid, Paul wanted to be a chef and so he went to culinary school. He grew up in the business since his family owned a restaurant in town that was popular, called The Golden Steer.

About 15 years ago Paul opened Paolo's, a wonderful Italian-gourmet restaurant. It's entertaining to watch Paul make each dish separately. There are no walls, so you can actually see him preparing the food. He's created a wonderful experience and is a fantastic chef. Over the years it's been fun to watch the progress of the business as it grew and flourished. Over those years he's done a number of wine maker's dinners, where a wine producer or owner will feature their wine, and might also include different wine pairings with different types of food. It's become increasingly popular with a lot of restaurants around the country, and it's a great way to keep in touch with your customers.

To celebrate the restaurant's 15th anniversary Paul came up with a cookbook, but was faced with the dilemma of sharing all his culinary secrets with his patrons, a situation similar to what I faced with my Client Camera Class. Did I really want to share all my secrets of photography with my clients? Did he want to share his tricks of the trade? On the other hand, they might enjoy knowing what you're making and learn to appreciate it that much more.

I had the pleasure of photographing some of the dishes for Paul's cookbook. It was a wonderful morning with him preparing the food and me photographing each dish, and then both of us sitting down and eating some of each dish, all in the course of just a few hours. The cookbook has been very successful for him, with proceeds going to a prearranged charity. It's another example of a great way to communicate. Educating your clients about what you do and how you do it, is a wonderful way of relationship marketing.

To take it up a notch, Paul is now offering cooking classes. I had the opportunity to witness first hand this great way of building relationships and staying in touch with your customers. When I arrived I was told what I'd be preparing and that there were two different entrees from which to choose to cook. I actually got to go into the kitchen and prepare it myself. This kind of hands on experience is the ultimate way to learn. Paul's a great teacher and treats you as a chef would treat an assistant chef with a little more authority than a normal teacher might. That is part of the fun and the experience, as well as being able to pair wine with the dish. His clients/students learn a great deal and then go home and apply what they've learned in their own kitchens. Once again, it will probably never be as good as what he can create in the restaurant, but their experience with him gives a new level of appreciation and will be remembered; through that memory, they will stay loyal to him.

H&H Color Lab
Customer service legends in their own time!

With any business or service, your suppliers can help or hinder your success. With a photography studio, the relationship you have with your color lab is essential. You can be the best photographer in the world, but if your lab can't process and print what you create in a timely manner, you're missing an opportunity to maximize your product potential.

I've worked with many color labs over the years—some okay, some good, and one that is outstanding. When changing labs, it's almost like going through a divorce. In the early 1990s when Sue and I started to travel more and teach throughout the country, we heard many stories about a lab near Kansas City, Missouri. These stories sounded almost like the stuff of folklore. Sue and I had never heard such praise for any supplier, let alone a color lab. In fact, they even had a waiting list to become a customer. What did this color lab do to create such loyalty? Read on and see for yourself.

In June of 1993, Sue and I lectured in Texas for the first time. The Professional Photographers of Texas organization is the largest state group in the country. Texas photographers are very pro-active and extremely hospitable. Our program was on marketing, studio management, and sales. It was a full-day seminar and it felt great when we finished and headed to an authentic Texas barbecue. After having an awesome meal, we were invited to join in a game of horseshoes. It was then that I met

RELATIONSHIP MASTERS

Ron Fleckal from H&H Color Lab. "Great program today," he said. "Thanks, I'm glad you enjoyed it." I replied. "You and Sue have a very similar philosophy about your client relationships as we do at H&H Color Lab," he continued. I said, "I've heard a lot of good things about your company; in fact, the stories are legend in our industry."

Ron began to tell us about the history of H&H and how its owners, Wayne and Shirley Haub got started in the lab business. "Wayne and Shirley are all about the relationship with their customers." Ron began. Sue and I looked at each other and thought, "That sounds familiar!" Ron continued, "You've probably heard we have a waiting list for studios. That's because we want to keep the standards high for the customers we have. Once we have a customer, we want to keep them for life." Once again, Sue and I looked at each other.

Within a year of that first meeting with Ron, we also became proud to say, "We use H&H Color Lab."

Developing a loyal following

In September of that year, we had the opportunity to fly to Kansas City and meet Wayne and Shirley and tour their facility. Wow! What an amazing operation. It was remarkable to see the evolution of their company, which started many years earlier in the Haub's basement. As our tour continued, we also got to meet the rest of the Haub family, daughters Kristin and Amy. Everyone made us feel welcome, and more importantly, like we were the only customer they had. This is the same sensation we felt when we first met Ron Fleckal in Texas. He was absolutely right when he said H&H is about relationships!

Putting the customer first

H&H does everything in their power to make their customer happy: getting orders out last minute, redoing orders no-charge, and listening to customers to further improve their business. In the photography world, it's always the lab's fault. That's who the photographer blames when the quality of work is not up to par. In reality, it's probably the photographer's fault: the image is under or over-exposed, out of focus, or a wrong setting was used on a new-fangled digital camera. The "artist side" of most photographers makes it difficult to admit to messing up. That's where H&H is a master at working with its customers. They recognize certain technical weaknesses with their customers and try to solve them in the lab, usually without the customer even knowing. Most labs will print what they get. I think the saying is, "Garbage in, garbage out." No matter the quality of work H&H receives, they turn out a first-class product for the customer. When you're an H&H Customer, you feel as though their doors are open just for you.

Investing in the customer

One of the most impressive things that H&H does is the way they invest in their customers. They spare no expense to educate the photographer on sales, marketing, camera techniques, and how to transition into the digital world. H&H has created their very own H&H University. This state-of-the-art facility has an incredible classroom, two sales rooms, a camera room (studio), and production area. Everything is first class, including the breakfast in the morning, snacks during the breaks, and wine and cheese at the end of class each day! What does this amazing university for photographers cost? Not one dime. It's part of being a customer of H&H Color Lab. I've had the pleasure of teaching there numerous times, and I'll tell you that each and every student feels so special being a part of the H&H family! The H&H University experience is the ultimate in relationship marketing.

Happy Holidays!

Another thing that has always impressed me about H&H is their generosity during Christmas. They don't just send out Christmas cards, but cards that have a selection of gifts that you can choose from. The value of the gift is based on your volume of sales for the last year. Among the goodies are educational DVD's and books, H&H gear, as well as $50.00 donations to charities like the Cancer Association. Who knows, maybe this book might be one of the gifts in the future! What a great way for H&H to say, "Thanks for the business this past year."

Dinner... anyone?

H&H travels to many of the photography conventions and trade shows around the country. You would think that their main mission would be to find new business, right? Wrong! It's to visit and maintain the relationships they have with their existing customers. There was a time in the history of H&H when you had to be on a waiting list before you could be a customer and even then they went to these trade shows. Once again, it was to nurture and maintain the relationship with their photographers in whatever part of the country they were visiting.

Most conventions are two to four days in length, and every evening the staff representing H&H rounds up a number of customers and treats them to dinner. My favorite part of the evening is when one of the staff stands up and says, "On behalf of Wayne and Shirley Haub and everyone at H&H Color Lab, we truly appreciate your business!"

Knowing Wayne and Shirley personally, I can tell you that they have a passion for showing their appreciation to their customers in the most sincere way possible. It's that type of attitude that has taken their business operation from a basement in their home to becoming one of the top color labs in the world.

Java Java Coffee Company
Building relationships through a drive-thru window
...one car at a time

As you know, the Pacific Northwest, specifically the Seattle area, is a real hot spot for coffee and espresso. This is mainly because Starbucks© originated here. You can't believe how many drive-thru espresso stands we have resulting in a competition that is extremely fierce. Brett Habenicht has been a good friend of mine and client for many years. In fact, he was a student at the high school where I taught. I got to know him as a student while he was in the choir and I was the band director. His mom was a secretary in the school office and therefore I got to do a lot of socializing with his family. Now I have gotten to know him as an adult and still consider him a good friend and colleague in the community.

Brent is a true entrepreneur. Coming out of high school he went into the navy, then got his real estate license and started selling houses as well as doing property development. Just as the espresso market started heating up in the mid 1980s Brett opened his first coffee shop, calling it Java Java. The interesting thing about this is that there was a lot of competition in the same shopping center but for some reason people always gravitated to Brett's place. His shop was very inviting and all the locals would be in there, talking about what they were going to do that day.

The coffee/espresso that he serves is phenomenal, smoother than most other espressos out there at the time. As Brett's business grew, so did the opportunity for him to expand. He started a few drive-thru's and found them as much, or even more profitable than having to lease space in a shopping center. So undoubtedly that's where he put his emphasis. As the years went by he decided, instead of purchasing coffee from a supplier, to invest in a coffee roaster. Within a few years, he had created such a large capacity of his own roasts, he decided to go into the wholesale coffee business. In doing that, he had his father go out and start researching who supplied all the restaurants and what supplier other espresso stands were using in order for him to work his way into that particular market. Today, just as I write this book, he has some impressive accounts, including IKEA, as well as many restaurants in the Seattle area. The quality of his coffee has granted him the reputation of a boutique designer roaster of small batch and savory locally roasted coffee.

To build customer loyalty Java Java began using punch cards. Buying nine coffees and getting the tenth for free. This was a great concept, something the big chains had never offered. This was a way he could effectively compete with the larger chains and reward their customers with great stuff.

Today Java Java uses very expensive, internet-based loyalty system that connects all the stores together so they can share information with each other and with the home office. The computer collects and gathers all the customer information. Brett's dynasty serves roughly 1,500 customers a day. The information gathered allows them to continue to keep in touch. When the cards are given out, Java gets their first and last name, email address, and sometimes their birthdays. This system allows them to market to that person on their birthday, by either sending them a free drink via direct mail, or automatically generated emails that say, "Have a free drink added to your account at Java Java Coffee, Happy Birthday! Those are the type of things that build loyalty."

The goal is to increase his personal customer mailing list by 20% in his data base, about 1800 customers. Brett usually doesn't use direct mail, because it's just a cup of coffee, so emails have been more effective. He tries to keep it simple, and his margins are so thin that it's really not advantageous, at least for his retail customers.

It's an entirely different story for his wholesale customers. He has higher margins on his coffee beans, but his wholesale customer list is only about 100, a lot easier to manage. They're buying his whole bean coffee and he wants to do whatever he can to reward them. In the last 16 years he's been able to develop relationships with a lot of different vendors and manufactures. One of the ways he rewards the wholesale customers is simple, a great example of Brett's philosophy is as follows:

> "If you were to call a repair guy and have him come out to replace the steam wand on a basic commercial espresso machine, it's going to be about $340. When our "big guns" out there give us a call requesting a new steam wand, I'll get out there personally and replace the steam wand at cost. It's a great opportunity for me to go out and show that customer, like IKEA, that they're important to us and that their business means so much to us that I'm willing to service the repair side of the business as well."

If you buy his coffee it will ultimately save you money, money you would spend of maintenance and repair. The coffee that you'll be buying from him basically could be a wash with what you'll save on new equipment, parts, maintenance, things like that.

That's been huge for Java Java! Brett has customers for 7-8 years now, which is really unheard of in the business. Typically when a customer leaves Brett, it has nothing to do with quality or price, but because someone has had a previous relationship with another roaster or simply gone out of business. It's not really a quality or price issue with Java Java; they know they're the best and they prove it everyday!

Benefits to the Customer

The biggest perk (no pun intended) for the customer is that Java Java has outstanding people taking care of you. Brett bases his hiring process on integrity, honesty, and commitment. He has great people that know how to build relationships through a window. He provides his customers with the very best employees he can find. These people know how to build relationships, friendships, and loyalty. That's a huge perk!

There are three big ideas that keep Java Java as successful as they are: quality, consistency, and service. Building relationships through a drive-thru window is difficult because you're not out there shaking hands and really embracing the experience. His employees are actually really removed from it—they're in a building, the customer is in a car. Building that consistency of having the same drink day after day is really important for his business, not only from shift to shift, but store to store...habits are comfortable. So that's one way to build a relationship.

Training his employees to be sincere with their approach to the customer is another way to build relationships and loyalty. They must not look at it as just a job, but an opportunity to truly make a difference. Maybe to us it's just a cup of coffee and another customer, but to Brett it's someone that has honored his business by not driving straight to work, straight home, or to another store or competitor. Those "potential" customers have made a special decision to stop and shop with him, therefore that choice deserves the same honor and loyalty they have shown Java Java. Brett has made a point to treat everyone as if they are his most important customer, and I think that's why his business has remained so successful in the community. Brett acts as a personal cheerleader for his customers as well as his employees by setting the example claiming, "You pass along good things, it doesn't cost anything to bring the right attitude to work with you, that's something that is so important!"

American Retail Supply
Educating your Customers

Keith Lee is a client of mine. I created his family portrait a few years ago during a gorgeous sunrise at his home on Lake Meridian in Kent, Washington. It turned out beautifully and now hangs proudly over his fireplace. Keith's business is about dummies... I mean Keith works with dummies... I mean Keith sells dummies. He's the owner of American Retail Supply, which supplies retailers such as gift shops, clothing stores, sporting goods, and pharmacies with everything from bags to bows, store fixture displays to mannequins, and everything in between. In the last two years, he's sold to over 26,000 customers! Keith has a huge passion for his business and an even bigger passion for marketing it. I never get tired of talking to Keith about innovative marketing ideas to his 26,000 customers. I invited him to lunch one day to learn a couple of his secrets. He's agreed to let me share them with you in this book. Thanks Keith!

Weekly Marketing tip

Keith admits to stealing this idea. Even though he has 26,000 customers in his data base, he doesn't have all of those customer's emails. But he does have, in his words, a "decent number". Here is his breakdown: He sends out a little over 9,000 emails per week and on average, only about 30% of them actually get opened. But still, that means that 3,000 people get his messages 52 times a year (including an additional message 26 times a year that may be something in particular he would like them to know). He does have a point when he says, "The biggest thing though, in my opinion, is that nobody **wants** to see your 'propaganda,' your 'special of the week,' 52 times a year." He does offer a special of the week down at the bottom of his Marketing Tip, that his customers really want to read. He has people that email him back and say, "Hey, my email was down. Can you re-send me your tip from last week?" Or, "I haven't got your tip for three weeks; I got back from vacation and there was nothing there." Keith reminded me of the old 20/80 rule: 20% of your customers provide 80% of your business. He's betting that the people who open that email are almost always those same customers. They're his 20% that give him 80% of his business.

Keith's response is not always huge to the special offer each month but he does admit that there are times when the response is pretty darn good! His biggest achievement is that he knows 3,000 open them consistently. So 3,000 of his clients, which he's pretty sure are his best clients, let him speak to them every week, which is incredible. If they need a dummy, who are they going to call? Mr. Keith Lee.

Client Appreciation Conference and Expo

Keith's other concept blossomed while attending a Zig Ziegler event in the early 1990's. As he sat there that evening, he thought "someday I need to do something like this for my customers." And thus, the Client Appreciation Conference and Expo was born. In the beginning his goal was to try and break even on the event, bring some great information to his customers, and create some long term good will. He brings experts in from a number of different areas, everything from direct mail marketing, tax and wealth, strategy, to internet marketing, to using a telephone in the retail business without driving people away. He also has a trade show with many of his suppliers showing the latest and greatest popular culture items. Believe it or not this incredible opportunity is free to all of his customers. In fact, he has a guarantee that states "this will be the best two days they've ever spent working on their business." And if it wasn't he would pay their airfare, hotel and meals. All they have to do is just come up to him at the event and ask for it if they were not satisfied. At his last event he had 800 people and not one person asked for their money back. Which was surprising since some of the customers who attended came from as far away as American Samoa.

To give you an idea of Keith's success story, I must mention that customers that came to his last event spent 98% more money with him than they did the year before. Now **that's** relationship marketing! Keith stressed to me one of the most important things in marketing: in our society everyone is taught not to brag about themselves. He doesn't believe in that whatsoever. What he's doing in his business, may it be his weekly marketing tip or his client appreciation conference and expo, is not bragging but making himself into a personality. People like to buy from people, he noted, they don't like to buy from businesses. He recalled an example at the expo where he had ladies coming up to him to hug him and tell him how wonderful he was. The reason for this pleasant show of affection was because he's allowed his personality to come through in his marketing. He's allowed his personal life to come through in the form of creating relationships. His customers who read his marketing tips or brochures inviting them to the conference know that he has two kids and they're more important to him than making money. As I mentioned before in the chapter about newsletters, it pays to personalize and not commercialize. By doing so, you bring your clients to a different level, where they're not just being satisfied by your product or service, they're a loyal follower of your business.

Keith appreciates all the relationship marketing efforts I do at the studio. He's a member of our Premier Portrait Club and receives all of our newsletters and E-newsletters on a regular basis. He recently gave a program to the Professional Photographers of Seattle on customer service. He mentioned to the photographers in the crowd how he received my newsletter every month. One member of the audience asked "Do you know how often Bruce mails those?" Keith answered, "I don't know, it seems like every month. The audience member knew it was only three of four times a year, but because of my relationship marketing, Keith felt as though it was every month, "Yeah, it seems like every month to me!" He complimented me by saying I stay in touch like no one else does in the industry "so, when my family needs photography where are we going to go? Not only are your portraits nice, but we know you're there, and we're not going to forget you." A very flattering comment made by a man who I consider to be a master at creating relationships.

Relationship Masters:
Doc Ingle

For some reason, I have a lot of clients that are dentists. One of them is Doc Ingle. What I admire most about him is his positive attitude and constant good nature. He surrounds himself with people that are, like him, very upbeat. The moment you walk into his office, you feel as though you're part of the family. It's the same atmosphere I have always wanted for my business.

Doc and his staff also have a lot of fun, even when they're working. I've had the opportunity to photograph Doc and his family throughout the years. I began photographing his two beautiful daughters for their high school senior portraits and then the whole family. He has a tremendous sense of humor, a little off the wall much like myself. To have some fun with his staff and his patients, he's created theme portraits that are displayed in his office. The first time he called, he said, "I have an idea for a staff portrait, and I want you to come and see what I have done in the past." So I went to his office to check it out and he had a portrait of his staff and he dressed up in a western theme, with an actual wagon trailer set up with horses. It was like something you would see in a western movie. It was interesting to see how they put that whole thing together. When talking to him, he said that his patients absolutely love this stuff. When they come in and look at the photographs they are able to relate to each of the staff members in them. As the years have gone by, I have had the opportunity to do a number of these for him. The first one I did was a golf theme. We obtained a golf cart and brought it to my studio back lot. I posed Doc and his staff around the cart dressed in golf garb. Doc was in the middle and actually laid across his staff. The finished image turned out wonderful and instantly became a hit in the office. These theme portraits have been an ongoing source of entertainment for Doc's staff and patients.

The most recent theme portrait started with a phone call from Doc saying, "I just bought a new Porsche, a white 911, and I have a buddy who has a black 911. So what do you think about me as James Bond and all the girls as Bond Girls? I'll be in front with a drill and we'll pretend like it is a gun, and name the shot, License to Drill!" What an awesome idea! So we booked the session and he let his staff know about six months in advance that they would be wearing slinky Bond Girl type dresses. Many of them started working out and getting ready for the shoot. Doc made it an enjoyable experience for the girls. They took the day off, got their hair, nails, and theatrical make-up done. Buy the time I got there to the location they were all looking great. Doc was in his tux and he carried a chrome plated drill. The staff does have one male in its ranks, a pretty tall gentleman at that. He was perfect to transform into the villain Jaws, from the "Spy Who Loved Me". Jaws was even equipped with a pair of chrome teeth just like in the movie. I set up the shot with the Porsche's and the girls with Seattle in the background. The session went smoothly and the image turned out remarkable. In fact it's my favorite theme portrait to date!

How does this relate to relationship marketing? Well, every time it starts when his patients come to the lobby. They are instantly entertained and amused to see their dentist play the role of 007, the golf pro, or him riding a Harley Davidson surrounded by Biker Babes." It's not something you're going to see everyday in most dental facilities! That's why it has such an impact. The best part of the Doc's relationship marketing strategy is that he sends the theme portraits out as holiday cards to his patients. That way he's actually giving everyone a piece of the portrait. Every time they see it on the fridge and show their friends, crazy Doc Ingle and his staff would come to mind. Now that's what I call relationship marketing! This year he sent over 4,000 "License to Drill" cards to his patients. He recently told me, "Yeah, it was a little more off-the-wall than we usually have done as far as a theme, but I tell you, I've gotten the best response from patients calling me, saying how much they enjoy it." The best part he said was that "A non-patient phoned me that saw the card at a friend's house. They asked to make an appointment and brought in both of their kids. I picked up a few new patients just because of this way we keep in touch and having a little bit of fun." Doc Ingle is a great example of generating creative relationship marketing and then sharing it with his patients.

Barrier Motors
"A Promise to do more"

I recently purchased a new vehicle from well known Seattle area dealer Barrier Motors, located in Bellevue just east of Seattle. You might recall me mentioning them in the "It's the Little Things" chapter. Barrier Motors provides free carwashes as long as you own one of their cars. My curiosity was heightened when I read their brochure regarding a Preferred Club. "What does it cost to be a member of the Preferred Club?" I asked the receptionist. "Nothing-when you invest in one of our cars your in!" she said.

One of my favorite marketing books in the 1980's that I have also mentioned in an earlier chapter is Customers for Life by Carl Sewell. Ironically he also owns car dealerships in Texas and Louisiana. Mr. Sewell continues to be a pioneer and leader in the customer service for his industry. Many of his concepts have changed dealerships all over the country. As I looked closely at Barriers B Preferred (B stands for Barrier) membership benefits, it was reminded of what I read in Customers for Life 20 years ago. Barrier, however, had taken similar ideas to a whole new and impressive level!

I loved the wording Barrier used as an introduction in the B Preferred brochure:

> *"The vehicles we represent sell themselves. Our role is to make owning one a joy. For as long as you drive the car you lease or buy from us, your B Preferred membership will assure you an unparalleled level of service".*

Here is the amazing list of benefits I look forward to experiencing with Barrier Motors:

- Loaner cars and service pick up and delivery with in 15 miles of the dealership
- Roadside service and mobile technicians
- Barrier license plate frame patrol
  This is amazing! If any Barrier employee spots a Barrier customer broken down on the side of the road, they will stay with them until the tow truck arrives!
- 90 day Barrier extended pre-owned warranty
- 7 day exchange on pre-owned sales
- Prompt shuttle service
- Online service scheduling and urgent care service
- Express oil change with no need to schedule ahead of time
- Loyalty and rewards program for repeat customers, service, parts customers, and referrals
- Customer care hotline
- Customer appreciation events and clinics
- Barrier Driving Experience, performance, and safety clinics
  Barrier connects with a professional racing school at a local race track. Customers can learn everything their car will do. They also provide a teen driving clinic as well.
- Preferred customer sales notices

- Free car washes at their state-of-the-art facility
- Free replacement bulbs and fluids topped off each visit, headlamps excluded
- Free first dent removal by the Dent Wizard
- Free Wi-Fi access at select showrooms
- Free trade evaluations
- Free tank of gas for each new or pre-owned automobile at time of purchase
- Special Barrier website access, email specials and entertainment opportunities

I had the opportunity to interview Michael Vena, one of Barriers managers, and was told some of the secrets of their world class services.

Q: Since this book is about relationship marketing, what percentage of your buyers are return clients/customers?
A: Probably in every sale, 60-70% are return clients. There are 2 cycles in our business: 2-3 year cycle for cars and then our core clients that will hold on to their cars for 6-7 years. Right now more than ever, most of our clients return every 2-3 years. We like that!

Q: When do you start the relationship process and how do you instill the need to build relationships with your staff?
A: There are a lot of things that you can say, but fundamentally, when a client/customer walks in our door, we make them feel welcome. It is not about making them think you care about them but that you *genuinely* care about them. People can sense when you're just trying to sell them a car. But when you really feel that you want to help them and they sense that feeling, you start building a long lasting relationship!

Q: What do you look for when hiring your sales staff?
A: We look for people that don't mind being servants, but mostly I want the sales people to have an honest desire to care for the client! At Barrier we have a saying- *Take an Interest, Not a Position. We hire for that type of Attitude!*

Q: Once you have sold a car and the relationship has begun, what are some strategies you use to keep in touch?
A: Our sales philosophy is that "You didn't get paid to sell a car. Your pay check was a down payment on taking care of that client."

Throughout the interview the message was clear. The relationship starts the minute prospective clients feel that he or she is not trying to be sold, but truly taken care of. This is such an elementary concept but powerful when it's implemented. Barrier Motors is an amazing example of talking the talk and walking the walk!

More than ever, Barrier is trying to partner with people in the community. By sponsoring and even hosting events, they understand the fundamental concept of being seen not as just another car dealership. Sounds like Win- Win marketing to me!

Q: Where do you get your ideas when it comes to servicing your clients?
A: We get our ideas from brainstorming with our staff and working closely with our advertising firm. The best ideas come from our clients- Just listen and they will always tell you what they want!

Q: Do you see any future benefits that will be added to the club?
A: We're always looking for things we can add- Some that can be considered out-of-the-box benefits.

Q: Like what for instance?
A: Our owner has a plane s likes to fly to warmer climates, like Palm Springs. Sometimes we will invite certain clients to join us. It is the ultimate use for Barrier frequent drivers miles! This benefit is a little tougher to let everyone know about, but we are working on it!

As a client of Barrier Motors I have to say that I am excited to be part of their family. I could have purchased my vehicle at numerous dealerships. It was the sincere and thoughtful sales staff, along with their dedication to customer service that convinced me to be a Barrier client. Working first hand it is obvious to me that relationships mean everything to their dealership. Mr. Vena sums this up by saying, "You have to take an approach and be very fair, but at the end of the day, your repeat clients do deserve special treatment, and there has to be value that's built in." Barrier's goal is to build its reputation each and everyday. Their catch phrase says it best, "A promise to do more."

12

FINAL THOUGHTS

I began this book project sitting next to the gorgeous Big Wood River in Sun Valley, Idaho. As you might recall, I had just finished an assignment that celebrated Blanche's 90th birthday. The party and family reunion was a beautiful ending chapter of Blanche's life. It's ironic now to share my final thoughts with you as I just finished photographing a 9 day old, definitely a chapter of the beginning of life! This session was extremely rewarding for me because the first time I photographed this brand new father, he was 4 years old…some 22 years ago. I recall, at the age of 4, he was not the easiest to work with. He, his brother, sisters, and cousins gave me a run for my money as I attempted to photograph his extended family of 24 people. His attitude toward being photographed really didn't change much during those 22 years. But despite the challenges I went through with him, he still saw the tremendous need and value for me to begin the photographic journey with his new born son! It was very apparent that his parents had instilled through the years the importance of quality portraiture and that it needed to be an investment in the family's heritage. Wow! This revelation hit's a bull's eye with the soul of this book! The relationship we had formed with this family over the years had transcended into the next generation. These lifelong customers became generational clients!

THE RELATIONOGRAPHER

As I've stated throughout this book, it's much easier and more cost effective to work with existing clients and customers than it is to always be looking for new ones. I learned this early on at my snack stand serving black cherry Kool-Aid to my repeat customers some 40 years ago! It's a concept I use each day with every piece of our marketing. From our newsletter, the Premiere Portrait Club, client camera class, and just a simple thank you, maintaining the client relationship is king.

The second half of the equation that will ensure success in relationship marketing is creating a memorable experience. May it be remembering names at Ivar's when ordering fish and chips, to having your own goldfish at the Hotel Monaco, to receiving car washes for life, we all have an opportunity to give clients and customers an excuse to come back. Being in the business of preserving memories and working with clients from their earliest moment to their final chapter, nurturing relationships though the years becomes extremely rewarding. I would never be able to put a price on watching the excitement of a father of a new 9 day old as I photograph his son for the first time, or the joy of a family as they celebrate the 90th birthday of their mother, grandmother, and great grandmother! I have the best job in the world! I guess it's all in a day's work for me, the relationographer!

I hope you've enjoyed my thoughts on the subject of relationship marketing and better yet are able to put them into practice in your own business! I look forward to meeting with you someday, possibly at a marketing conference or maybe in front of my camera!

Till we meet, bye for now.

To contact Bruce Hudson, the Relationographer, email him at:
brucehudson@earthlink.net, or brucehudson@relationographer.com,
or 800-952-6609.
Bruce is always available to lecture at any workshop,
convention or conference.

He loves to customize his Relationographer program for any type of organization from corporations to insurance professionals, from Mary Kay Cosmetics to realtors.